D0873019

Diary of a WWI Pilot

Harvey Conover, First Lt. 90th Aero Squadron, in U.S. December 1918, after his return from France.

Diary of a WWI Pilot

Ambulances, Planes, and Friends
Harvey Conover's Adventures in France
1917-1918

Presented by
Frances Conover Church

To Jim

Best Wishes

Frances Conover Church

11/15/09

Conover-Patterson Publishers

Diary of a WWI Pilot
Ambulances, Planes, and Friends
Harvey Conover's Adventures in France 1917-1918
Presented By Frances Conover Church
Editor, John Church; Cover Design, Scott Poole

Publisher's Cataloging in Publication
Church, Frances Conover
        Diary of a WWI pilot: ambulances, planes, and friends:
        Harvey Conover's adventures in France 1917-18/Frances
        Conover Church
        p. cm.
        Includes bibliographical references and index.
        Library of Congress Control Number: 2003096941
        ISBN 0-9653071-3-1
            1. Conover, Harvey

Conover-Patterson Publishers,
P.O. Box 8647, Spokane, WA 99203-0647

In loving memory this book is dedicated to
my parents Harvey and Dorothy Conover
and to my brother Larry and his wife Lori.

ACKNOWLEDGMENTS

This book reflects the collective effort of family members, friends, as well as helpful strangers contacted in the Meuse area of France in 2002. Of course the principal author is my Dad, Harvey Conover, who diligently recorded his adventures and left an exciting personal history of World War I during the years of 1917 and 1918.

As publisher and editor my husband John Church designed and laid out the book. We gathered and verified information regarding locales, the ambulance service, flight and aerial gunnery training, ground and aerial combat, and individuals mentioned in the diaries. Chronologies were added for those readers wishing to relate diary entries to what was going on in WWI at the time. We are particularly grateful to Scott Poole, graphic designer, publishing expert, and author,who created the cover, maps, and helped with the book's design, and production. Kelly Howard, whose courses increased our knowledge of Photoshop, also provided specific computer guidance.

My late brother Harvey Conover, Jr. in addition to recalling many experiences with Dad, contributed many photographs, articles, and letters. My daughter Sarah Conover and stepdaughter Sally Church Petersen reviewed and made suggestions for my Preface and Afterwards material. Cousins Dick Conover, Polly Frank Shank, and Isabel Storer Vandenberg, went back into their archives and found many old photographs and letters that helped tell Dad's story. My son Richard Gagney, daughter Carolyn Conover Curtis, and friends from my childhood Peter Guest and Johnny "Pete" Peterson recalled their personal memories of Dad for the Afterwards section.

Our research was greatly facilitated by friends who provided books relating to World War I. Thomas E. Talkington, Colonel, US Army (Ret), made available to us many useful books on World War I from his military library. Warren Schneider kindly made available an important source of maps and battle descriptions related to the diaries, *American Armies & Battlefields in Europe,* prepared by the American Battle Monuments Commission in 1938. We appreciate the permission granted in a letter from Anthony N. Corea, Colonel, US Air Force (Ret), Director of Operations and Finance of the American Battle Monuments Commission, Arlington Virginia, to republish portions of maps and text contained in this reference.

The browser Google provided a frequently traveled path to a rich lode of internet information related to the diaries. Some of the most useful on-line sources are listed in the Bibliography.

In the small village of Ourches, on the Meuse River south of Verdun, local historian Lucien Vainerot and his wife Monique opened their home to us and shared their photographs and maps of a nearby airfield where my father was stationed in France in 1918. At the Memorial de Verdun in Fleury we were given special attention by the Assistant Curator, Elisabeth Sauvagnac-Rodier who shared photographs and books with us. Our trip to the front line locations near Verdun and the memorials erected to thousands of valiant men from France, England and the United States made a lasting impression on us.

EDITOR'S NOTES

This presentation of Harvey Conover's 1917 and 1918 diaries is based on a word for word transcription, modified to accommodate the requirements of printed page layout and readability. Frames have been placed around the headers of pages containing material from the original diaries. Some of the many symbols and truncated words Conover used have been replaced with full length words. Paragraph breaks have been added in some longer entries. French words and phrases, particularly those related to ambulance service or flying, have been italicized and a French-English Glossary placed at the end of the 1917 Diary section. An effort has been made to verify the correct spelling of people's names and places. An index of such names and places may be found at the end of the Appendix.

France 1917-1918 Diary Locales

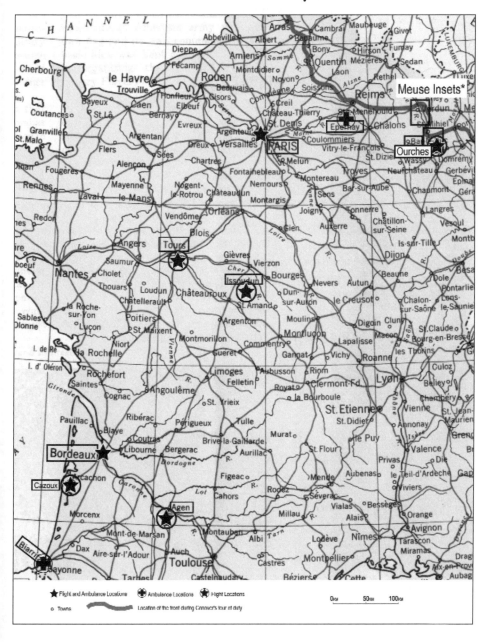

Contents

Introduction

I. 1917 Diary

II. 1918 Diary

II. 1918 Diary(Cont.)

Introduction

Dad was faithful in his journal writing. He wrote two diaries about his experiences in World War I during the years of 1917 and 1918. The 1917 diary is a small maroon, leather-bound book worn thin on the edges. The 1918 book is black, about the same size, equally worn. Penned on the inside cover are the words "Harvey Conover, First Lieutenant A.S.S.C. USR, U.S. Air Service, A.E.F. France. In the event of the above party being bumped off kindly forward this book to Mr. & Mrs. L.P. Conover, 51 So. Oak Street, Hinsdale, Ills."

I spent a summer copying the still legible but yellowed and faded handwritten pages. I discovered within these pages a remarkable sweep and breadth of experience. World War I comes alive in his day-to-day writing. He records a time of great patriotism, many fatalities, periods of seemingly interminable waiting, training, combat, and personal discovery. His 1917 diary begins on March 6 with his saying good bye to his folks and friends at the railway station in Hinsdale, Illinois. The second book ends with my father, a medal-bedecked hero, on crutches with a knee full of shrapnel, at a crowded veteran's hospital in New York City on January 7, 1919.

He volunteered for the American Ambulance Field Service months before the United States declared war on Germany. When he arrived at the front, he drove his ambulance through rough terrain, sometimes during gas attacks, picking up the wounded, often with shells exploding all around them. Many times, he worked through the night to bring the injured-both

French and German to field hospitals.

During a leave in Paris from ambulance service at the front, he signed up to become a pilot in the American Air Service. He was "itching to fly" and get into the fighting at the front. He received flight training from the French in Tours and Issoudun. Assigned to the 90th Aero Squadron, he flew combat missions over the front lines in the San Mihiel-Verdun area.

In World War I, combatant nations began for the first time to give aircraft a significant role in their battle plans. It was a time for experimentation. Initially planes were used for observation, next bombs were carried and dropped on ground targets. Pursuit planes, equipped with machine guns, began to engage in aerial combat. Aircraft were unreliable: wings fell off, motors failed, throttles stuck, and much too often, the planes would crash. Yet, there was no problem recruiting young soldiers to fly. A great feeling of camaraderie grew among the pilots and their observers.

During 1917, Dad seldom missed a day of recording his adventures. He shares his feelings, which changed a great deal during the two years. He enjoyed the diversity of the soldiers from many countries. He grew to admire the courage of the French. He loved seeing new places, making new friends, and learning new skills. He savored his time in Paris, enjoying the city's flavor and attractions, its café's, and especially the French women.

His views shifted as he saw many of his friends and acquaintances wounded or killed,. He expressed hatred for war and the Germans as he saw shells wipe out hospitals, towns, and villages leaving maimed and dead. The diaries include the names and descriptions of friends and acquaintances killed or missing in the war, how they died, and the admiration he felt for them.

Later, he seldom discussed his wartime experiences with his children. A few of his strongly expressed negative comments and criticisms have been omitted as they conflict with his views when I knew him. I do not think he would have wished them to be included.

Dad was a man's man: patriotic, competitive, resourceful, fun loving, and eager for action. He relates a unique history of the First World War, which I found, reads with the thrill of a novel. It conveys a depth of human experience about this period seen through the eyes of a twenty-five year old. I think you will find it as memorable as I do.

Frances Conover Church

Harvey Conover dressed as a pirate at a University of Wisconsin party, circa 1916.

WWI Events 1914-1915

1914

June   Archduke of Austria assassinated in Sarajevo.

July   Austria declares war on Serbia

Aug.   Beginning of WWI: Germany declares war on Russia when it supports Serbia; Germany declares war on France & Belgium; Great Britain declares war on Germany; Wilson proclaims U.S. neutrality; Serbia declares war on Germany; France declares war on Austria; Great Britain declares war on Austria; Japan declares war on Germany.

Sept.   First Battle of the Marne begins. Trench warfare starts with Battle of Aisne.

Nov.   Ottoman Empire declares war against France, Great Britain, and Russia.
Battle of Falkland Islands. First German air raid on Britain.

1915

Feb.   Germany announces war zone in British waters. Franco-Anglo Champagne offensive begins, ends in March with heavy losses.

March   First passenber ship, the Falba, sunk by Germans. Allied naval attack on Dardinelles.

April   Second Battle of Ypres begins with German use of gas. British landing on Gallipoli. Field Service of the American Ambulance begins front-line operations with units in Alsace and Dunkirk.

May   Lusitania sunk by U-boat off Ireland. Italy declares war on Austria-Hungary. First Zeppelin raid on London.

June   Isonzo offensive begins on Italian front.

July   Wilson directs Secretaries of War and Navy to draft a defense program.

Aug.   Warsaw captured by Germans. Sulva Bay Offensive at Gallipoli.

Oct.   Allied troops land at Salonika, Greece.

Dec.   Haig made commander of British Expeditionary Force.

WWI Events 1916

1916

Jan.   French occupy Greek island of Corfu. Austrians occupy Cettinje, Montenegro. Zeppelins bomb Paris and English towns.

Feb.   Britain enacts conscription. First Battle of Verdun begins with German offensive. American Ambulance Section moved to Verdun. Fort Douaumont falls to Germans.

March   Germany and Austria-Hungary declare war on Portugal. Sussex, French steamer, sunk by U-boat. Melancourt taken by Germans.

April   Wilson warns Germany not to pursue submarine policy. Irish rebellion in Dublin ends in week with surrender of leaders. British force of 9000 surenders to Turks at Kut-el-Amara.

May   Cymrio, White Star Liner, torpedoed off Ireland. Austrians over run Italian positions. British gain Vimy Ridge. Bulgarians invade Greece. British and German fleets in Jutland naval battle.

June   Russian Brusilov Offensive begins. Lord Kitchener lost en route to Russia when Germans sink British cruiser off Scotland. Germans capture Fort Vaux in Verdun. King Constantine orders demoblization of Greek army in response to Allied demand.

July   Start of Anglo-French Somme Offensive. Longueval captured and Pozieres occupied by British. British and French advance.

Aug.   French recapture Fleury. Italian Goriza Offensive begins. Roumania declares war on Austria-Hungary. Italy at war with Germany. Germany at war with Roumania. Hindenburg made German Chief of Staff. Bulgaria at war with Roumania.

Sept.   Bulgarian forces invade Roumania. Italians defeat Austrians on the Corso. First use of British tanks as British capture Flers and Courcelette on western front. Roumanians retreat from Transylvania.

Oct.   French recapture Fort Douaumont at Verdun.

Nov.   Germans evacuate Fort Vaux. Woodrow Wilson re-elected. Somme Offensive ends. Austria-Hungary Emp. Franz Josef dies.

Dec.   David Lloyd George made British Prime Minister.

As the quick transportation of wounded — from the front to the nearest hospital — is so great a factor in saving their lives, the American Ambulance Field Service was organized soon after the beginning of the war, and during the subsequent two years its achievement has fully demonstrated the value of its purpose. It has now in the field more than 200 motor ambulances. These are driven by young American volunteers, most of whom are graduates of American universities. *To them has been successfully entrusted the vitally important matter of bringing the wounded in the shortest possible time from the trenches to places where the first surgical help can be given. Upon this first surgical help largely depends, naturally, the chance of the wounded surviving long enough to reach the base hospitals.* These ambulances are grouped in sections of twenty to thirty cars, and attached to the French Armies. *They carry wounded between the front and the Army Hospitals within the Army Zone.* So valiantly has their work been done that in each section a number of these men have been given the *croix de guerre* for gallantry under fire.

Owing to the fact that five new sections of ambulances have recently been sent to the front, the waiting list of the past eighteen months has been depleted, and accordingly a limited number of

Volunteer Ambulance Drivers are Wanted

New men are also needed from time to time to fill the places of those who return to America on leave, or who are unable to re-enlist at the expiration of their six months in the field.

REQUISITE QUALIFICATIONS

American Citizenship — Good Health — Clean Record — Ability to drive and repair Automobiles — Sufficient Funds to assume Travelling Expenses.   (No salary, but living expenses paid.)

For further details and terms of service apply to

WILLIAM R. HEREFORD   or to   HENRY D. SLEEPER

Headquarters American Ambulance,   c/o Lee, Higginson & Co.,

14 Wall Street, New York   State Street, Boston

Excerpts from a folded sheet bound inside back cover of *Friends of France: The Field Service of the American Ambulance*, Houghton Mifflin 1916 found among Harvey Conover's books.

1917
War Diary

WWI Events First Half 1917

1917

Jan.   Britain intercepts telegram from German Secy. of State
        Zimmerman to German Minister to Mexico instructing him to
        propose German-Mexican war alliance if U.S. ceases neutrality.

Feb.   Germany resumes unrestricted submarine warfare. U.S. severs
        diplomatic relations with Germany. Franco-British Conference
        of Calais unifies Western command.

March   Mexico denies receiving Zimmerman note. British capture
        Bagdad. Russian revolution begins. China breaks with Germany.
        Czar Nicholas II abdicates. U.S. ships City of Memphis, Illinois,
        Vigalencia, and Healdton torpedoed.

April   U.S. ships Aztec and Missourian sunk by torpedoes. U.S.
        DECLARES WAR ON GERMANY. Cuba and Panama join
        war as U.S. allies. Austria-Hungary and Turkey break with U.S.
        Arras offensive begins. First use of tanks by France. Lack of
        coordination and losses at Chemin des Dames precipitate a
        French "military strike," labeled mutiny by the press.

May   Petain replaces Nivelle as C of C of French armies. Foch
        appointed Chief of Staff. Wilson signs U.S. conscription bill.
        Pershing made commander of AEF.

June   Draftee registration begins in U.S. Battle of Messines begins:
        British advance at Wytschaete Ridge. Greece declares war on
        Central Powers. U.S. enacts Espionage Act. First U.S. troops (1st
        Division) arrive in France.

Harw Conover's Diary

Starts March 6, Chicago Ill, U. S. A.
— 1 9 1 7 —
ENDS — GAWD KNOWS WHERE.

This is an attempt to describe
the experiences exciting and otherwise;
personal and impersonal also the
impressions and opinions of one
damn fool who left an ideal
home surrounded with luxuries and
a possibility of business successes in
search of that most attractive
phase in the lives of the human race
known as Adventure.

In case of the death
of the writer kindly send
this book to
Mrs.+ Mr. L. P. Conover
51 So Oak St
Hinsdale Illinois

HARV CONOVER'S DIARY

STARTS MARCH 6, CHICAGO ILL, U.S.A.
ENDS - GAWD KNOWS WHERE

This is an attempt to describe the experiences exciting and otherwise, personal and impersonal also the impressions and opinions of one damn fool who left an ideal home surrounded with luxuries and a possibility of business successes in search of that most attractive phase in the lives of the human race known as Adventure.

In case of the death of the writer kindly send this book to
Mrs. & Mr. L.P. Conover
51 So Oak St
Hinsdale, Illinois, U.S.A.

March 6, Hinsdale and Chicago

A.M. in Hinsdale--Goodbye to Folks--Noon 12:30 Club. Mack, Chick, Juby, Rach, Shrimp, and Dad down at Station. Butts, John and I bound for Washington--argue war and sin in observation car until threatened by other passengers

March 7, Washington, D.C.

Perfect day--Ride thru Alleghenies very beautiful. Passed great many coal mines.

Arrive Harpers Ferry in afternoon, Washington 5:45. Butts bargains with taxi driver, arrive at rate of $1.00. Same at Hotel Winston, which is a dump. Eat at Harveys Restaurant, famous for seafoods.

March 8, Washington and New York

Rise 8 a.m. Breakfast and contract with Sight Seeing Bus. Go thru US Pension Office where a lot of inaugural balls are held & which is largest brick building in world. Bureau of Engraving print bills and stamps 25,000,000 per day. New Natl Museum most interesting collection--Congressional Library very beautiful building. Listened to Senate debate Filibuster Bill and international situation. Sherman seems to favor Germans. Excitement over our relations with them and possibility of war very noticeable. No one allowed to carry cameras thru buildings. All suspicious characters closely watched. Most interesting city--greatly

impressed by the slow movements and methodical habits of people. Leave Wash 2:45 p.m. arrive NY 8:00 p.m. Take in Maxims
and other cafes.

March 9, New York, NY

Spend day as follows: Go to Herefords office 14 Wall St--get passports and letters of credential. Have passport visaed by French
Consul. Lunch at Del Monaco's--"Highway Robbery." Get ticket at French Line and check trunk. Try to see Liners but all
guarded. Return to Hotel. Go to a dance at Hotel Plaza.
Florence Myers, Cousin from Rochester, Butts and his girl, John
and I. Music best ever heard--time most enjoyable.

Eat dinner at small French restaurant Table d'hôte just off Bdwy
very good. Butts, John & I go to Hippodrome, Annette
Killerman's dives, scenery, and show great. N.Y. the only place in
country where such a spectacle can be seen.

People here are greater hustlers than Washington DC, but all
are robbers and money seems to be the only thing that counts--
Have encountered no sentiment. The man with the "Jack" is the
only one that counts

March 10, New York, N.Y.

A.M. Letters and Postals. Johnnie, Butts & I lunch at Kaiser
Keller. Butts went out to see his girl. Johnnie & I went to Beta
House at Columbia U. very small, not many there. Went swimming in University Pool. Talk with Coach Jamison-Columbia
team very good.-College Buildings very elaborate & well built--

gym well equipped, but school entirely lacking in college life and spirit. Later in afternoon John and I call on Flo Myers--Butts and his girl there. Take dinner down town. New York lights in theater district and crowds most impressive sight due to great prosperity & beautiful warm evening.

March 11, New York

A.M. Rain-Went down town, Johnny & I ate lunch at Table d'Hôte. Evening quite large--Met Butts and Margaret Gibbons in Wallick Café danced there until one then went to Healies which stays open all night.

March 12, Embark on SS Rochambeau

Logged 261 miles. Morning spent in making arrangements to sail. Sailed at 3:30 p.m. SS Rochambeau. Our stateroom is two decks below, which might prove inconvenient. Johnnie, a man named Butler, & I in same room. Butler is expert mechanic on his way to serve in France. Passengers made up about 2/3 ambulance men, 1/3 French soldiers returning after furlough, elderly men, and a few women-about 200 in all. Directly at sundown, all windows and portholes were carefully covered to exclude all light on account of subs. Our dinner tonight was of the French style, wine instead of water but no butter or milk. The bread was of the sour Vienna type. A fresh off shore wind is blowing and the ship rolls slightly causing some apprehension among landsmen. This is really the beginning and is greatest ever.

March 13, SS Rochambeau Second Day Out

Logged 360 miles. The wind has freshened into a norwest gale.

Our course this morning was northeast but we have now shifted to a more southerly direction. The ship rolls so much that it is very difficult to walk & at dinner tonight not a few dishes were spilled and broken. There are 75 ambulance men aboard. Everyone is a live wire and a fine fellow. A fellow from Texas eats on my right while at my left is one from Massachusetts. About one half of the passengers are sick—several leaving the table tonight mid the laughs of the rest. So far I feel tip top.

I am not able to realize that we are aboard a belligerent boat, that the soldiers aboard are returning to fight, perhaps to be shot, and that at any moment we may be torpedoed and sunk by a German submarine. The portholes are closed and covered at night excluding all light. We have a gun mounted at our bow and stern and the lookout keeps a very sharp watch, otherwise there are no signs of war. We all laugh, talk, sing, play cards, and enjoy our-selves with no thought of the danger, which is always present.

March 14, SS Rochambeau Third day out

Continued rough weather course shifted to SE direction. Day spent in reading, eating, sleeping and chewing the rag. Had a talk with a French Soldier who on his arrival in France is going to try to get in the aviation. When I spoke of danger was calmly informed that he did not care if he was killed. This spirit seems to run among all the French. I seem to be catching it myself, as the thought of being torpedoed does not bother me in the least. Nearly all of the passengers are the same way & refuse to let the thot of danger spoil this trip. Tonight we all sat out on the lee deck and had some close harmony, which lasted until ten thirty.

Then Johnny & I each drank a stein of beer and turned in. I have my sheepskin coat, sweater, flannel shirt, pants, bottle of whisky and compass tied together and placed at the foot of my bed, which is two decks below, so I will be able to exit with a certain degree of celerity.

March 15, SS Rochambeau-Fourth Day Out

Wind continued strong and northwest course throughout day SE. Among French Soldiers aboard is an aviator who has three decorations & who is the crack shot of France. He amused us this a.m. by shooting ashes of a cigar held in another soldier's mouth – distance 30 feet. Sea very rough. He holds the record of bringing down three boche aeroplanes in 20 minutes.

Ran around deck a.m. then took salt bath. Read and fooled around in p.m.

 Evening spent as usual rendering plenty of harmony on lee deck & retiring with customary stein.

About the food: We have red & white wine instead of water, at least two meat courses, usually three, always salad and fruit, coffee or tea. We all eat so much that it is a wonder we can get around & if this is the way France starves, lead me to France!

We sighted a schooner this p.m. the first ship of any kind since leaving NY. We are evidently zig zagging well out of the regular route. Last two days my compass has been pretty steady tho no subs sighted.

March 16, SS Rochambeau-Fifth Day Out

Course still SE. Wind shifted from NW to SE blowing strong. Johnny has very bad cold, coughs incessantly- called on Fr. Dr. this a.m. and went to bed.

The wind has increased to a gale and looks like an old fashioned equinoxial storm is with us. Large crap game in saloon stakes often as high as $50--not for yours truly.

I met Miss Katharine Baker, woman of about 33 on her way to do Red Cross work, cousin of Woodrow Wilson. Quite an interesting woman, very well up on politics. Inquired of "Jamais," our cabin steward about the boches but was duly squelched. It seems that the French and Germans are not on friendly terms.

March 17, SS Rochambeau-Sixth Day Out

Course still SE blowing gale, very rough, no one slept last night so day was spent that way. Usual song on deck after Dine- Nothing exciting happened.

March 18, Rochambeau-Seventh Day Out

Course SE wind less strong sea subsiding. Spent a.m. reading, p.m. in smoking room. Grand relief auction and entertainment held by Boat after Dine. Program consisted of singing, card tricks, acrobatics & Heffren recited Nellie Match Girl, which was quite a hit. Auctioned everything from champagne to cigarettes, all of above articles given by passengers-raised 3600 francs. Ended up by singing Marsailles. The spirit of the French is really wonderful when you think of what they are going thru & see their apparent good spirits-it seems incredible. They are giving everything they have & do it cheerfully. A French woman aboard the boat told me of her husband wounded in the Hospital in Paris & of her son whom she is returning to see before he goes to the first line trenches. He is 20 years old. Her bitterness toward the Germans is really terrible.

March 19, Aboard SS Rochambeau-Eighth Day Out

Course SE Sky Overcast, Sea Calm.

We are now in the restricted submarine zone and both our bow and stern guns are uncovered, loaded, & manned. An extra sharp lookout is being kept but no subs have been sighted.

Have been listening to stories of German atrocities which seem incredible-bayonetting babies, inoculating prisoners with tuberculosis, & cutting off the hands of boys that they may not be able to carry a gun. These stories come from French witnesses & German diaries.

Had quite a chat with Miss Katharine Baker who feels so bitter that she implores everyone to kill every German he saw in any way possible. These things seem to be beyond human credence & if true every German in Germany should be wiped out.

Our speed has been greatly increased & we are now entering the danger zone.

March 20, Aboard SS Rochambeau-Ninth Day Out

Course SE Moderate NW wind-Full speed ahead.

We are now well in the danger zone and are cramming on full speed. This afternoon we had a life boat drill and the boats were left swinging from the davits to be of instant access. Two men are now watching from the crow's nest and not even smoking is allowed on deck. We sighted eight ships going west this p.m. Appeared to be English Transports. The conversation of the passengers has now drifted to submarines as the principal topic. Some are planning to sleep on deck tonight. Our cabin is three decks below & only one exit leads to same, however, if this is blocked, we can probably get out of the porthole on a very tight squeeze.

We expect to sight land tomorrow-probably coast of Spain altho our position is known only to Captain.

The harmony quartet will not be allowed to assemble on deck tonight which is certainly hell for the other passengers. Here's hoping tomorrow brings forth some excitement.

March 21, Aboard SS Rochambeau

Keen watch kept all day but nothing happened. We sighted the coast lighthouse at eleven p.m. and expect to take on our pilot early tomorrow morning.

I had quite a talk with Rockwell, a young American returning from a furlough to the front. He is in the American Escadrille and he's now been flying for over a year. His brother was killed some time ago while flying. The aviation game surely must be interesting & I itch all over to get in it. However, I learned that it costs about $20 per month which makes it extremely difficult. Something may turn up to help matters 'tho on our arrival in Paris. Here's hoping.. I wrote several letters to U.S. this afternoon & evening was spent as per usual.

March 22, Aboard SS Rochambeau (Left ship, Bordeaux)

We picked up our pilot at 5 a.m. and just in time too for we had gone right into the middle of the French mine field which had been moved since the departure of the Rochambeau. A destroyer came out & saved the day. If we had struck one of these mines with our bow loaded with dynamite & ammunition, it would have made a most lovely mess. We anchored in the river until two p.m. waiting for the tide & arrived in Bordeaux at 5 p.m. In the meantime our passports were examined & several men advised to see the police. Our baggage was gone thru but nothing taken. We have located in La Hotel Teircrious for tonight & leave for Paris tomorrow as there is but one train a day due to the war. Johnny & I went about a bit this eve and certainly had an awful time trying to make ourselves understood. The streets are filled with soldiers and nearly all the women are in mourning. All lights are put out at 9:30 p.m. even the streetcars stop running at that time.

Sherman was very much right when he said war is hell & the conditions even here in southern France are pitiful.

March 23, Bordeaux to Paris

Heffren, Johnnie, Byron, Hath, & I rode up in one compartment the Imperial Quintette. Country surrounding Bordeaux slightly rolling and covered with vineyards. The fields are being worked by the women, old men, & children, practically no young men or men can be seen except those in uniform back from the front on a short furlough. The country is already very green & trees are beginning to blossom, the brightly painted farmhouses & chateaux of stone, which have stood for generations make the effect very beautiful. The roads are very twisted & seem to run in no definite direction but they are all very smooth and exceedingly well kept. We saw very few automobiles due to the fact that they have been requisitioned for the front, the two wheeled carts drawn by one horse & escorted by a woman or child are very much in evidence.

Red the Killer from Montana has broken out with quite a rash and says he feels fairly rotten. Red is some boy.

Arrived Paris about 9:30 p.m. and were met by ambulance and driven to our quarters. I drew a bed in the tent.

March 24, In Paris

Nearly froze last night but so did the rest. Army cots don't seem to be overly comfortable at first. Spent morning in registering & signing our lives away to the Paris Police. Ate down town & ordered uniform in p.m. Spent evening seeing the sights.

Paris is under very strict military discipline. All lights are extinguished at 9:30 p.m. when all shops are closed & even the subways, streetcars, & elevated, are not allowed to run. Each day certain few articles can be sold & amusements are open. Three nights a week the theatres can run. Three other nights the cafes can remain open etc. up until 9 o'clock. About one out of every seven street lights is on, giving just enough light by which to make your way. The elevators do not run in the buildings & a tax is levied on almost everything taxable.

The crowd on the streets is made up of men in uniform, women in black, and very few civilians dressed as in times of peace. It makes you feel like a slacker to walk in this crowd without a uniform & will sure be glad when mine is made.

March 25, In Paris

We are quartered in a chateau & annex with about 60 fellows because of delay in getting chassis up from Bordeaux. The chateau has been given to us by Countess De Hottinguere and is a most interesting bldg. facing the Seine with some very fine gardens. Secret passageways run from the chateau to the Seine It is said to have been occupied by Voltaire & to be of some historical significance.

Our meals are plain but good & we have plenty of everything but butter & none of that. The bread is hard and stale. There is also very little sugar.

Stuart, Byron & I took a walk down the Seine this a.m. We passed the Eifel Tower, a large number of galleries, & other famous bldgs. We arrived at the Cathedral of Notre Dame just in time for mass. It is the most magnificent building I have ever seen. The number of things to see in Paris seem to be limitless. My greatest regret is that most of the art galleries etc. are closed to save coal necessary for heating them. Coal is now $80.00 a ton.

This eve was a theatre night so we went to the Follies Bergere-Costumes were wonderful but acting not up to our musical comedies. Great many of the tunes played were old American popular tunes.

March 26 - Paris, Monday

I spent most of the day working on the old cars. In the evening we went to the movies--Admission $.20. Saw several vitagraph pictures about four or five years old. Also one French humorous picture which would never have gotten by in the States. Mrs. Cortis would have died. The intermission in the middle of the show was 15 minutes & everyone went back to the bar, which runs in connection with the show, & had a drink.

The ticket takers & streetcar conductors are women. Even most of the guards in the subway are of the female sex, but they seem to take care of their jobs in good shape. The Paris subway system is very good & by transferring you can get to almost any part of the city. The fare is $.03.

March 27, In Paris

Went down town for my uniform in p.m. but it had to be altered. After a great deal of searching we found Henry's Bar which is the hangout of the aviators & ambulance men. It sure did seem good to see Americans all around us & to be able to order a drink without trying to speak a lot of French.

This city is not laid out in any systematic fashion but it just grew. As a result it is very difficult to find your way & you very easily lose all sense of direction. We have been lost several times & usually have a very hard time finding places. The streets are nearly all narrow and crooked run into courts where they stop & pick up in some other direction.

We went down to the Latin Quarter in the p.m. & went in several of the famous cafes where we saw the long haired artists drinking their wine. We were unable, however, to find any apache dances.

March 28, In Paris

Continued rain. I have not mentioned it before but it has rained here every day since I arrived. The result is a most uncomfortable cold & clammy temperature inside as well as out, for we have no heat in our quarters, coal being almost as valuable as diamonds. Another important thing I have not mentioned is the women. They are the prettiest I have seen anywhere. They all have beautiful complexions and very few are not in someway attractive, most of them are beauts. We have the time of our lives trying to converse with them & the amount of pep they have is wonderful. The French all seem to have very sunny dispositions and are almost always smiling & laughing.

March 29, In Paris

Still raining–I got my uniform today & feel a great deal better able to go down the street without being considered a slacker.

I went over to the Hospital at Rue Bayonne & saw Miss Grace Gazette a relative of Mrs. Rockwells, this p.m.

She makes all kinds of apparatus for soldiers who have been crippled to facilitate the uses of the injured member & correct it as much as possible. She is quite famous and receives cases given up by the greatest French Doctors. Her systems are original & may revolutionize this type of treatment. She is also a very fine & attractive woman.

This evening Byron, Hath, and I went down town-looked in Maxims & Henry's but did not have much time on account of the 9:30 closing law. This city once the gayest & brightest in the world is now without sufficient illumination to walk easily along the street.

March 30, In Paris

Showers all day. Drove around the city a bit with Mr. Fisher in a.m. P.M. John and I went down town. Looked up Haigh at Amer. Radiator. He is a friend of Roy Makemsons & has been over here for some time. He showed us some of the new places & we returned to the Chateau for dinner. Evening spent in reading & talking about the fire.

The cafes in Paris impress you more than anything else there are some on every block and they all sell liquor. The Frenchman goes to one of these places orders one drink & stays all afternoon talking and watching the people. This is his chief form of recreation. When he is young he spins a top and rolls hoops. As soon as he grows up, he spends his leisure in the cafes.

March 31, In Paris

Showers during the day. A.M. Hathaway & I went down town. Went out to Versailles in p.m. Passed the old city wall & moat, the remains of which remind you of the tales you hear of France in the olden days. There is a very large military encampment at Versailles & I must have seen 1000 motor trucks lined up in front of the barracks. Companies of soldiers marched back & forth. With the castle at the end it made quite a sight.

In the evening, we went about the cafes whose patrons at present are nearly all soldiers on furloughs. The women who frequent these places are in very sorry straits owing to the absence of tourists and number of men at the front. Therefore we were very much sought after by a great many & the situation was novel if nothing else.

April 1, In Paris

Continued rain--weather most gloomy. P.M. went down to hospital & gave Red the Killer some books. Spent balance of afternoon walking down the boulevard. Men from every part of the globe (except Germans) were on the boulevards in uniform & it was surely a great sight. This city at present is filled with the most cosmopolitan group of men in the world.

War is a fine thing in some ways but in others is terrible. I saw a boy about seventeen years old this afternoon minus one arm & with half of his face blown off. The man that comes out with a whole body, however, has an invaluable experience. I had an interesting talk with an English woman who has four brothers in the war. Two are aviators & one took her up in his machine over Paris. She describes this flight with no fear & says that she is afraid of nothing, which I think is true.

April 2, In Paris

Continued rain. James McConnell of American Aviation Corps & Suckley of American Field Ambulance were both killed a week ago. I attended their memorial services this morning in the American Church & was greatly moved by one of the best talks I have ever heard. The Church was filled with Americans, Ambulance men & aviators, also a few men and women in civilian clothes. In all of our hearts, there was nothing but praise for these two men who have died in such a wonderful way.

In afternoon Byron, Hath, Foster and I went out to the contagious hospital with a bunch of magazines for Red Woodhouse who has been out with measles, chicken pox or something & nobody to talk to. Fussed around a bit in eve & went to bed.

April 3, Paris

Continued Rain and Snow. Throughout all of this weather we have had no fires in the house & there is not a man without a cold. I had my driving test this morning before the Prefect of Police & am now in possession of a chauffeur's license in Paris for life.

Johnnie & I went roller skating this afternoon at Luna Park & had a great time. I made the acquaintance of one peach of a little French girl who could not speak one word of English. I had my dictionary & we carried on our conversation with that. Have a date for dinner tomorrow. Her name is Madi Petit.

Talked with a man who has just come in from Switzerland. More tales of German atrocities from the exchanged prisoners in that country. Those people seem to be nothing better than animals.

April 4, Paris

Continued rain--Hathaway & I went thru the Louvre this a.m. that is we walked about the gardens, all of the buildings are closed & the pictures taken down to avoid them falling in the event of a bombardment from Zeppelins.

I met Madi in the evening & took her to dinner. She picked out a restaurant where not one person including herself could speak English & I had a hell of a time. It was one of the funniest experiences I have ever had, our conversation was carried on by means of my pocket dictionary. But that woman doesn't have to talk, just let her smile.

When I returned Johnnie, Foster, Byron & I made a raid on the wine cellars which are in the underground passageways & sat on a wine vat used centuries ago drinking wine that was in a big barrel & had been there for one long time cause it sure had a kick! After a few we were able to sing plenty & the whole thing turned out to be the funniest party I have ever been on.

April 5, In Paris (U.S formally declares war)

Raise the flag. We saw the sun all day. The U.S. has formally declared war on Germany & a great many American Flags are flying about town. We have become noticeably popular & the French seem to feel that our entering will shorten the war considerably.

Haig called up this evening and invited me down to the Café de la Paix where he, his wife & I sat until 9:30 closing time. They have been over here a year and like it very much. This city seems to grow on you and there are many ways in which the French people are far superior to us.

Last night was Thursday so the subway ran until 10:30 p.m. It does this only on Thursdays, Saturday and Sunday, which are the only nights. All other nights all cars stop at 9:30 p.m.

April 6, In Paris

Another nice day. We saw quite a few aeroplanes and one French dirigible this a.m. Went to church, this very good Friday, at the Madeline, which was built by Napoleon. The faith is of course Catholic and the form of worship new to me with a great deal of kissing of a piece of bronze. The altar was filled with flowers molded into the shape of a cross with a most beautiful painting reaching to the ceiling in the background, giving a most beautiful effect. The sides of the altar were filled with a myriad of candles.

We also had a nice evening & the imperial quartet assembled in the garden.

April 7, In Paris

Damp, overcast & uncomfortable. We went out to the hospital at Nuilly this a.m. It was, before the war, intended for a big school, but luckily, the interior had not been completed & it was immediately turned into a Hospital and run by volunteer Americans. It is from this base that the Paris Ambulance, which at this time has 40 cars, operates. Eighty-three *blessés* arrived this a.m. and they have been very busy.

Since yesterday's final declaration of war the town is covered with American flags and we are all very popular. Dr. Andrew thinks that the U.S. will allow no more men to come over for ambulance work, & I am sure glad I left when I did for guarding munition factories or bridges in the U.S. does not seem particularly appealing.

April 8 In Paris

Perfect Day. Went to church in a.m., that is the American Church, and listened to a sermon by a mumbling minister. In the afternoon Foster, Johnnie, & I went thru the Palace & gardens of Louis XIV. The whole effect is wonderful & the gardens, fountains, & artificial lakes give the most beautiful effect imaginable. It is from this palace that the mob took Louis XIV & in 1870 where the German French Peace treaty was signed.

The skies about Paris were filled with war planes, which are becoming so common that we scarcely look for them any more.

Red the Killer arrived tonight from the hospital & we all went down to the Rotuvel Café in the Latin Quarter, which is filled with the most mixed crowd I have ever seen. We all had a very enjoyable party.

April 9 In Paris

Snow, Rain and Sunshine

Monday. I met Madi at 2 p.m. went to Cafés & sure had a great time. Am now able to speak French like a Parisian (not)- Big Evening. It's a great life if you don't weaken. In my absence Johnnie & Byron got wind of trouble from A. Piatt Andrew & went up to see him. Report as follows: wine had been stolen from the cellars by the men in the tent. They had stolen eggs, etc. from the kitchen. Killed and cooked one of the Countess's chickens, etc., etc. Things looked most black, but they finally smoothed the troubled waters & result a most clean, orderly, & quiet tent. I will not venture to say how long this will last cause we sure have a wild crew.

April 10, In Paris

Rain, Snow & Clean.

Day spent doing very little besides clean tent, bathe, and play catch. We heard today that Germany refuses to admit that we are at war with them which is sure good.

A new section goes out tomorrow or the day after, made up of the men who came up on the Chicago. We will probably get out in about a week, and altho I am having a great time here, am mighty anxious to get out to the front.

April 11, In Paris

Usual wetness in bunches. Went down to the old part of Paris this a.m. with Stout and Harris. We saw the palace once occupied by Francois I & his Courtiers, the home of Alexander Dumas, and several buildings erected as far back as 1545. This district is far from the public byways & we were great curiosities in the eyes of the natives who gathered about us in a big crowd when I took a picture saying to each other "Les Engles," which made us mad but American are scarce. Section XV has its banquet tonight and leaves for the front tomorrow. It is composed of the crowd that came over on the boat before us.

I feel now as tho I had lived in France all of my life & am enjoying everything. Am afraid this wanderlust & adaptability to different places will never leave me.

April 12, In Paris

Thursday. Fooled around all day and accomplished nil. Have very bad cold which certainly makes you mad & pepless.

Met Madi in early dinner & roller skating, now can understand most of what she says, and I have come to the conclusion that is some way to learn French.

These French women are sure wild and full of pep. I used to think I had a little pep, but when it comes to competing with them, I'll throw up the sponge.

Arrived home to find that the gang had been slumming at the Petite Poulles & were thoroughly disgusted. Dick Stout, when he heard that the bunch had gone, got out of bed, dressed, & took a taxi down.

Hathaway had been to another party & was very funny. "Cold as a Frog. Why should the spirit of mortal be proud."

April 13, in Paris - Nice day

Friday. Fooled around in Quarters Latin in a.m.

P.M. went down to the Hospital for the blind & helped print some books for them in raised type. The press is run by hand & very tedious. It is a terrible sight to see the blind soldiers grope their way about the courtyard, they are all educated men & deprived of their former means of livelihood.

The big scandal about Paris is Navarre--Before the war he was an Apache. He entered the aviation & a year ago was the idol of Paris. He is an ace & has brought down 7 or 8 Germans. About a week ago he went into a theatre drunk and raised hell. A French officer asked that he be evicted but he was told that the man was Navarre & they refused to arrest him. The officer then went over and tried to stop him. Navarre knocked him cold. He was then put in jail and he told them he wanted to go out & fly so they let him go & he went out & killed a couple of Germans. Then nothing was heard from him until yesterday when he appeared down the main street 40 mi per hr in his machine. He ran over seven gendarmes killing 2, some of them ran up on the sidewalks & he went up after them, he missed & turned around & came back after them. Then he went out, got in his aeroplane

& disappeared. Some think he went to Switzerland others Italy.

April 14, In Paris

Saturday–Nice day. I found out today that I am one of the lucky ones to go down to Bordeaux & drive up a chassis. I leave at 8:00 this eve & will arrive tomorrow a.m. Six of us in a 2nd class compartment, no sleeping facilities, 11 hours to Bordeau. Harris and Fay slept in the two clothes racks & the rest of us draped ourselves about the compartment. I tried to sleep half on the floor & half on the seat. Well, we managed to get in an occasional snooze & altho the night seemed like at least a month, we came out alive & the experience was sort of different. As the Frenchman says, *C'est la Guerre.*

April 15, A.M. in Bordeaux, P.M. Bound for Paris via auto

We got our flivers in shape in the a.m. They consist of a chassis with an improvised seat on it, which is sure hard. There are about twenty cars.

At 2:30 we departed on the road to Paris & certainly passed thru some beautiful country. The road is winding, smooth & lined with trees on either side, already in bloom. The fields are rolling & covered with vineyards. All buildings are of stone & we passed an occasional chateau. The towns are very compactly built & front right on the sidewalks of high uninviting walls. Behind these walls are courtyards, but they an inaccessible from the street. A French soldier drove at our head showing us the way & two mechanics brought up the rear. We arrived at Ingletering, a town built on the top of the hill by evening & are now in the

Hotel de Paris.

April 16, On Road from Bordeaux to Paris

Monday. Slept like a log till 8:00 a.m. & went down in the court to find a flat tire. Breakfast of fried eggs & chocolate. You can't beat the French chocolate & again got underway. The weather was perfect & we wound our way down thru the town, which covers a very high hill out into the country.

France is primarily an agricultural country. We saw practically no factories & the towns are merely distributing centers. The people live in a most primitive way and even the best hotels in the larger towns are far behind ours in modern conveniences. Things considered necessities in the U.S.A. are luxuries here. Of course conditions are now bad on account of the war but living conditions are always easily discernable.

In the middle of the afternoon I had to drop out of line for gasoline & as a result fell somewhat behind. I opened up wide to catch the line & held the fliver at about 45 miles per hour until she froze solidly & had to let her cool before I could even turn the motor over. This happened three times before we caught up & sure had a wild ride. The rest of the day was spent in racing each other & if we get in whole gawd will sure be with us.

April 17, Driving from Bordeaux to Paris

Today was not as pleasant as we were occasionally obliged to drive in a cutting rain. But as this trip is not intended for pleasure or a Cooks Tour, we had to stick it out.

In the middle of the afternoon, while driving behind Byron Harris, I saw him look around, his car struck the edge of the road & threw him out then turned a right angle & plowed into the opposite ditch bending the wheels and smashing the front axle. Luckily Harris was only bruised, but we had to leave the car at the side of the road to be picked up later.

We stopped at the next town, filled up with essence & bunked at the hotel. Cold, hungry and tired. The town, altho of considerable size, was very quiet & men of a military age were decidedly conspicuous by their absence.

April 18, Bordeaux to Paris

Arose to find it raining hard, ate breakfast and went over to the Cathedral of Chartres, which is far more wonderful than Notre Dame and is recognized as the most wonderful gothic cathedrals in the world. It was filled with elderly women in black praying, I suppose, for their absent ones at the front & of course for a safe conduct on their own young. A big priest occupied one of the altars. He was dressed in a most gorgeous white robe & mumbled a quantity of Latin. It rained like the devil all day & on our arrival in Paris, we were absolutely plastered with mud and grime.

De Wordener, our manager, smashed his car just a few miles out of Paris by running into a bearded Frenchman. It seems that he was asleep & did not see the Frenchman signal to stop. Anyway each blamed the other. Went down to the Latin Quarter in eve & had a good time with probably the most cosmopolitan collection in the world.

April 19, Paris again

Went down to the Invalides–thru Napoleon's tomb and the museum in connection with the grounds. They have enough junk in the museum to keep one busy for a month. The tomb is wonderful and most impressive. His body was brought from St. Helena after being interred there for 19 years.

Met friend Madi in the evening & took in the usual schedule. Am now able to understand a great deal of French and if I could be here a couple more weeks feel sure I would be able to rival the true Parisians.

April 20, Paris

Johnnie & my names were posted this a.m. for Section 16. Harrison and Hathaway were not on, which sure makes me sore.

Our cars are ready and we depart. Monday, but do not know as yet for what part of the front.

Went out to this park this afternoon where they assemble our ambulances and make aeroplanes. The aeroplanes are sure pretty and they make a fellow nutty to get into the aviation service. You have to serve six months in the ambulance first tho. I intend to put in my application tomorrow. I can't imagine a better life than sailing around in the clouds. Altho it is of course necessarily short.

April 21, Paris

Saturday. Johnnie & I went up to Galatti this a.m. & asked to be put into the next section because of the fellows in it. Straight with Galatti gets mad & now our chances to get out are similar to the celluloid cat in Hades.

Took a walk thru the park this p.m. and met a French girl who wanted us to translate a letter from an English Tommie. We did so with the aid of a pocket dictionary & it sure was good. We also ran into a bunch of boys playing soccer, refugees from Lille, who invited us to participate. Well we entered & they ran rings around us and enjoyed it. Went out with the Mademoiselle in the evening.

April 22, Paris

Today the entering of the U.S. into the war was celebrated & we marched down to Washington's monument two abreast. At this place they played the Star Spangled Banner & made several speeches ended by singing the Marsallais & yelling vive la American. We then marched down town & were cheered all the way. I guess they don't realize how little we have done. The entire city is flying the American flag and one has been run to the top of the Eiffel tower right beside the French flag. This is the first time such a thing has been done in history. I sure hope that quick action is taken by the people at home & that they realize the seriousness of the situation.

April 23, Paris

The time is now beginning to drag a bit and I am getting mighty anxious to leave for the front. Our section is expected to leave next Friday.

Johnnie & I went up in the Ferris wheel this afternoon, which gives quite a view of Paris. We also walked thru the Tuilleres Gardens and talked over everything, deciding the fate of the universe. I bought a soccer football.We intend to assemble a team as soon as the section departs and challenge all comers.

Received a special delivery letter from the woman saying that she would be unable to meet me ce soir, which ended the day most unsatisfactorily.

April 24, Paris

Saw Section 16 leave yesterday and had a game of soccer football.

Spent the afternoon working in the garage, and the evening wandering about. The weather has been perfect today, and it sure seems good to be warm again.

The Parisians are all heaving a sigh of relief as it now looks like the cold weather is over, and last winter was the worst ever experienced. It was bitterly cold and the majority of the people had no way to heat their houses. The suffering was really terrible.

April 25, Paris

A.M. Down town after eluding friend Anne who was searching for volunteers to load chasses. Strolled down the Boulevard de Italias and took in the sights in general.

Today a restriction has been placed on all meats and absolutely no meat can be served in the evenings. This leaves lunch as the only meal in which meat can be had. Spent the evening with the Madam.

April 26, Paris

One day is getting to be very much like the next now. We get up in the morning about eight o'clock in time to make breakfast, fool around and amuse ourselves without a care in the world. It sure is great & I have come to the conclusion that war is not all hell.

We had our farewell banquet this evening, which was composed of plenty of good food & champagne. Dr. A. Piatt Andrews presided and we had short talks from Prof. Marle Baldwin, The Abbey Dinant, A French Captain and several other Frenchmen of note.

We are to leave here Monday morning and drive to Bar-le-Duc where we will attach ourselves to a company & follow them wherever they may be detailed.

April 27, Paris

The weather is great and has been perfect for the last week. We were allotted our cars this a.m. and became acquainted with our section leader. His name is Neftell & has been with Sect IV for a long time. He is about twenty-four years old & seems to be a mighty nice chap.

Four of us went over to the Y.M.C.A. tennis courts & played doubles all afternoon. The courts are perfect & they furnished us with both racquets & shoes, which was A 1. The Y.M.C.A. in Paris is just being started by a couple of young fellows who up until the declaration of war had been working among the German prisoners in France. This work will now continue under the auspices of the Swiss.

April 28, Paris

Saturday. Spent the day getting my things together to take to the front. In the afternoon Johnnie and I went down to see Dr. Gros. He is in charge of the enlistment into the American Escadrille. We both feel, now that the U.S. has declared war, that we should take a more active & effective part in the war than the Ambulance. The American Aviation Service offers about the best opportunity so we underwent the necessary physical examination and filed our applications. There is a possibility that we will be drafted out of this service before our six months is up depending upon the demand for pilots. Here's hoping we will be. Spent the evening and dinner with our French girl & said good bye. Guess it is a good thing I am leaving Monday as things are getting sort of intricate.

April 29, Paris

Today we learned that conscription had been adopted in the U.S. It seems that they are coming to over there. I sure am hoping this is true.

Went down to the Latin Quarter this evening for one last farewell party in the old Rotund. Sure had a great time and altho Shorty O'Brien & Brownie were pinched by the gendarmes, they were let off and the evening was a big success. The gang of us locked the spirits in our cars after climbing over the garden wall.

Forgot to say that six of us went swimming in the Seine in the afternoon. The regular bathhouses were not open so we undressed in a barge & went in our underclothes. The water was sure cold & the current so swift that we could scarcely swim against it. A crowd of Frenchmen gathered around, but they think all Americans are crazy so were not surprised.

April 30, To the Front

Went to Porter's funeral in the morning. He came over with us, contracted the measles and died. Mighty nice chap. The services were in the American church and consisted of singing and reading-most unsatisfactory I thought. Such superstition ought to be placed at a minimum and a good straightforward talk supplemented.

We all got underway at 3:30 p.m. left Paris and got started for the front. We stopped for the night at Pantene, a small village a short way out of Paris. I have one of the French mechanics riding with me. He can't speak English so we try to converse in French. We stopped in the Town Square & pulled our cots out in the open & undressed in front of the mob of onlookers, who did not seem to mind & sure had a good sleep. Hathaway got mixed up with some Frenchman & was beaned on the head with a pipe, but we got him home all right & the wound is not deep.

May 1, To the Front

We are certainly getting some wonderful weather. The sky is without a cloud & the temperature ideal for driving.

We made Meaux by noon, which is as far as the Germans got on their first drive. We then reached Virtus about 8 p.m. where we had a dinner consisting of corned beef, coffee, & bread in a dirty little café. Virtus is a very old town & like most of its type is dirty & has no modern conveniences such as running water. The lavatory in the restaurant is connected with the dining room so the odor is most unpleasant.

The country is rolling, well cultivated, & beautiful. Everything is green & the roads are perfect.

We now pass many companies of soldiers & the roads are crowded with military motor trucks. We could hear aeroplanes flying above us both in the day & night. We slept in our cars & believe me I slept.

May 2, Bar-le-Duc

Another perfect day–Today we passed through the Champagne district into the Argonne. The fields are now dotted with graves flying the French flag, showing where a trench of soldiers lie. A great many of the houses in the villages lie in ruins as they have been left by the bosche shell fire. The roads are filled with trucks and we pass companies of soldiers of every nationality. This war seems to be a business, all efforts are to its needs and it seems to have gone on always.

We arrived at Bar-le-Duc, the distributing centre for this part of the front, at 3:30 p.m. and finally settled in the outskirts for the night. We all then went swimming in a nearby canal and attempted to get rid of some of the dirt with which we are covered. The ride throughout the day was one of the most beautiful and enjoyable I have ever taken. I am lucky enough to be leading the convoy so get less of the dirt with which all are covered and a fine opportunity to see everything.

May 3 Bar-le-Duc

Today we settled at a suburb of Bar-le-Duc and were atttached
to a division which is now being organized about us consisting of
15,000 men. We are camped on the grounds of an old estate
about 50 feet from a cold, swift mountain stream in which we
take a plunge every morning. The estate is on the border of a
very small village about 15 kilometers from Bar-le-Duc. It is certainly beautiful with its quaint bridges, shady walks, and green
pine trees.

Tonight there is a full moon, not a cloud in the sky. Of course
the quartet had to assemble. We can hear the faint boom of the
big guns from here, otherwise you would think we were in some
pleasure camp. The surrouundings could not possibibly be better unless we had a lake and a couple of sail boats at hand.

May 4, En Repose

This morning we all washed our cars and cleaned up the camp
generally as we are to be inspected by the General tomorrow. In
the afternoon Byron, Johnny, Shorty, and I went to Bar-le Duc
with Neftell & the Sergeant. We stayed in, had dinner, saw the
town & walked back. The roads were stationed with soldiers and
altho they are not supposed to let any one pass after 8 p.m., we
encountered no trouble, and even examined one of the sentinels
guns. Arrived home about 10:30 p.m. & dumped all the fellows
out of their cots onto the ground. A general roughhouse ensued
but there were no casualties.

May 5, En Repos, Bar-le-Duc

The General of our division inspected us this a.m. and seemed to be very well impressed. He asked each man his age, business, or what he was doing then shook hands with him. This is quite unusual with Generals & is considered very much of an honor.

At dinner our Lieut. passed around the champagne in honor of our inspection & celebrating the news that we are to move up to Dead Man's Hill in a few days.

Neftell, our Chief, Hathaway, Harris, Johnny, Brown, the Killer, & I sat around a table in a dirty little restaurant drinking champagne & beer until midnight. One candle was our only light. The windows were closed & covered as it is against the law to serve drinks after 8:00 p.m. We all sang, bulled, & radiated good cheer. The family of French sang some of their songs for us & the whole party proved that it isn't the place, but the company that makes the time. When we arrived at the tent we all stripped and did some fancy diving off the bridge. It was raining & the water was like ice so it was not as pleasant as it sounds.

May 6, En Repos

Last night a boche airplane flew over Bar-le-Duc and the people all ran into the *cave voûtés*, which are very well filled at such times. The antiaircraft guns were turned on him but no damage was done.

We went to Bar-le-Duc in the afternoon & fooled around a bit, but returned for dinner and hit the hay early.

May 7, En repos

Worked on our cars in the morning and in the afternoon Roughe Foster and I took a walk to Ligny, a town six kilometers from our camp.

We received word today that we are to move up in the vicinity of Dead Man's Hill on Thursday. This sure is welcome news and Thursday can't come any too soon for us.

We all went down to the hole in the wall this evening & spent our last cent. The quartet assisted by the entire company rendered most wonderful harmony & after we arrived home we dived off the bridge. It was as cold as a frog in a frozen swamp if you know how cold that is.

May 8, En Repos

Went foraging in the a.m. procuring a table, benches & a quantity of wood from a springhouse in the hills. The country about here is most beautiful: everything is green and wild flowers are growing everywhere.

We fooled around with the football in the afternoon & not finding any excitement in the evening turned in early.

The people in the Provinces are not as attractive as the Parisians and the women are nothing compared to those in Paris. In fact, that city seems like an altogether different unit contained people of another race.

May 9, En Repos

Wednesday. Arose at 6:00 a.m. & went to town with the Commissary department in search of food. The French Armies are certainly terrible for red tape, and it required all of the morning to procure our necessary food for our journey tomorrow.

We met a Frenchman who had been a cook at the St. Francais Hotel in San Francisco & a banker from Rio de Janeiro. This country is filled with men from all parts of the globe.

May 10, To Vadelaincourt

We left Guirpont at 9:00 a.m. and drove up the famous road to Verdun over which for three months 50,000 motor trucks were driven both day & night. The villages we passed thru are in a half-rebuilt state & everywhere are ruined buildings & houses smashed by boche shells. The hills are covered with old French trenches and the fields spotted with graves.

We arrived at Vadelaincourt, a small French village now overflowing with soldiers, in time for lunch & officially attached ourselves to our division which is still in repose. This location occupied by the French is surrounded on three sides by boche trenches, the nearest being a distance of about 10 kilometers away.

A boche plane flew over in the afternoon & it was a most beautiful sight to see the shells from the antiaircraft guns break around it. A Frenchman finally went up in a Spad & brought him down. He was so close when he shot him that he could see the blood run down his face.

May 11, At the Front

We are located on an aviation field & each evening 20 aeroplanes leave, fly 200 miles into Germany, drop bombs & return. We can never look about us without seeing 2 or 3 aeroplanes & they are becoming more numerous than flivers in the States.

Walked out to some rear line trenches this afternoon where they were practicing the art of throwing hand grenades. It was necessary to duck down in the trenches when they exploded as they throw iron & steel in all directions & explode about thirty feet away. These grenades are very powerful & it is most dangerous to pick up one that has not exploded as the slightest jar may set it off.

May 12, At the Front

We walked to Verdun today, a distance of 15 kilometers. Saw a number of trenches with barbed wire entanglements. Nearly all of the houses in Verdun are demolished and no one is living there.

In the evening after a game of baseball the Lieut. took the quartet over to see the aviators. Their quarters are luxurious compared to those of the ordinary military men. One wall of the living room is entirely covered by an oil painting of a night scene in which a number of birds are flying above the aviation field. Each bird's head is the likeness of one of the aviators. The effect is most unique.

We sang a couple of songs which seemed to amuse them because of their newness. They passed around champagne which they had flown to Bar-le-Duc for (50 kilos) the night before and sang to the accompaniment of a piano taken from Verdun.

They are a fine crowd and certainly have a lot of pep. As one said, "Laugh & sing and die tomorrow." That certainly is the way to live.

May 13, At the Front

Sunday. Football, that is Soccer, Section 17 vs French Aviators at 4:30 p.m. Final score 2-2 and some game. Our team lacked the finer points of the game & we were handicapped by many fouls made thru ignorance as very few of us had ever played. We bettered them in condition & strength, however, & with a little practice could easily whip them. Thruout the game you could hear the boom of the guns, & several boche aeroplanes were being shot at above us. Our audience was composed of officers, soldiers, & nurses.

The war is the most common thing out here. It is an accepted & necessary evil very seldom spoken of.

After the game, we were all treated to the beers at the quarters of the aviators.

May 14, Front

Lay around practically all day with a sprained ankle received yesterday in the game. We started a game late in the afternoon of baseball. It was interrupted, however, by a heavy thunderstorm. We all stripped & stood out in the rain receiving our first shower bath at the front.

This is certainly the laziest life in the world and I am afraid we all will be good for nothing from now on. In the army, you lie around for four weeks and fight for two. We are lucky, however, to be quartered at the front where things are going on until our division is fully made up and we can be busy.

May 15, Front

Played baseball in the afternoon and went over to see the aviators in the evening. We are now getting pretty well acquainted with these fellows & have a lot of fun with them. They showed us a large number of pictures taken at a height of 4000 meters. Telescopic lenses are used & the results are wonderful. One picture in particular, a photograph of a city in Germany, was so clear that you could make out the most minute detail.

An escadrille nearby takes these pictures in the daytime. They are then passed over to our friends who study the location of the places to be bombarded then go out at night & drop their bombs. One aviator also showed us an evil looking knife that he carries to be used on the boche in the event of being captured. If I were the boche, I would shoot him from a distance only.

May 16, Front

It rained most of the day nevertheless; we pulled off a soccer game with the Interpreters, who are mostly English. They beat us 2-1. I was unable to play on acct of a sprained ankle rec'd in the game with the aviators. Will be o.k. for the next game, however.

One day is becoming very much like another one, and altho we are seeing a great deal, we are all anxious to see the rest of our division come up so we will have some work to do.

May 17, Front

There is a large cemetary adjacent to us. The bodies are thrown into a large deep pit, dirt is thrown upon them. Crosses bearing their names & French insignia which consists of a circle of red & white, very similar to a target. An occasional grave is more elaborately decorated & on closer inspection, I found them offi-cers. Several aviators are also buried in this place. They too are accorded a greater honor than the *poilus.* A small part of this vast expanse of graves points diagonally toward the east. These are Turcos who have come from France's colonies to die for her & never to return to their homes so far away. Their last request is always to be buried with their feet facing to the eastward & the rising sun.

Quartet met in the evening. Also plenty of crabbing because we have not had more to do. Can you beat it?

May 18, Friday, Front

McMurry has bought a little fox, which makes 3 dogs, & a fox in our repertoire of mascots. No one has bought a young pig yet, but several are thinking of it. The chief drawback is a lack of funds. This is the most broke & least flush gang I have ever been with. We all live in the past. The days spent in Paris. I now have not spent a cent for two weeks. The reason for this is that I have not had it to spend. Today passed very much like the rest. Nothing exciting happened.

May 19, Front

Johnnie & I took a ten mile walk in the rain this a.m. It cleared off in the afternoon, however, & we started a most exciting baseball game. At the end of the fifth inning, it was broken up by the appearance of a boche aeroplane directly above us and the breaking of antiaircraft shrapnel all around him. The German exhibited the greatest amount of nerve. Two Frenchmen started out to get him. He, instead of turning tail faced the music & dropped bombs all around us. Then after sailing about some more, pointed leisurely for home. Furthermore, in spite of the shrapnel & French he got home. The praise lies decidedly for the boche.

May 20, Front

We played the Electricians this afternoon in a game of soccer. They had the best team we have struck. Their captain is the best player in France. They got the jump & scored four goals in 15 minutes. We then tightened up & final score ended 4-1. Our tactics were the roughest they had ever seen & they were very much of a bunch of cripples by the end of the game. They did not ask us for a return match.

On arriving home, we discovered that we are all in a state of quarantine. One of our Frenchmen has come down with spinal meningitis. This sure is hell & means a week on our tails in this spot when we expected to get into action in a couple of days. Neftie is going to try to shift us to another division and here's hoping he can do it because this medicine chief is most efficacious & disagreeable.

May 21, Front

The whole French front seems quiet and everyone is anxiously awaiting developments. The usual crap game reigned supreme and in as much as yours truly is still broke he lost no money.

This quarantine is sure getting on our nerves nothing to do but lie around and the bunch is getting crabby.

It rained very hard last night. My corner of the tent collapsed on me and Jack Rue & I were forced to step out without clothes & brace it up.

May 22, Front

The medicine chief together with his staff examined us for spinal meningitis by taking most elaborate samples of our throats.

Played some baseball in the afternoon. The game, however, was a continual grouch and fight. Evening same as usual.

May 23, Vadelaincourt

Coupez a Frenchman in our section was a former resident of Belgium. When the boche occupied his city, he hid in the garret of his house. His wife & children were taken. He has not seen them since. He then sneaked out of the city and made his way toward France. He traveled by night & hid by day. Finally he succeeded in getting thru the boche lines and is now fighting for France. For this action he was today decorated by the French gov't. We all attended the ceremony and congratulated him.

Champagne was served at lunch & all gladly drank to his health.

Rumor started in the evening that we were to be ordered to paint our flags off of our cars because we were a part of the French Army. The largest indignation meeting that you have ever seen immediately ensued & we all swore that this could be done only over our dead bodies. The air was blue–then we learned that the rumor was false.

May 24, Vadelaincourt

Baseball-quarantine lifted in the afternoon for which we were all duly thankful.

The night proved to be clear and good for bomb dropping. The escadrille adjacent to us does this type of work only. Tonight four of these machines flew over boche lines to drop bombs on a pack train being brought up.

The greatest danger incurred by these men is landing which is extremely difficult even with the aid of the searchlights, which are thrown upon the field. It is necessary to be going at a speed of 60 mi per hour so any miscalculation proves disastrous. When the aviator wishes a light, he shoots a colored rocket. He is then answered by his field by a system of lights. If a hostile plane is near he is not allowed to come down, as the lighting of the field would expose them to his fire at every great disadvantage. However if everything is clear he is given the signal, the field together with the guiding lights on the hill is illuminated & he swoops in. The field is again left in darkness.

May 25, Front

The evening was perfect. The temperature ideal & the sky perfectly clear. It was also a good night for an air raid & fifteen planes left the hangars, flew over the boche lines to a large shipping & railroad center, dropped their bombs & returned. One plane was hit by shrapnel but he succeeded in getting back over the lines where he was forced to land without the aid of searchlights. Unfortunately he hit a tree & fell. Their luck was miraculous. The pilot was only bruised & the observer cut & his arm broken. They fell near Verdun & we sent an ambulance over to pick them up. After watching the rest swoop in we hit the hay.

May 26, En Repos

Today very much like yesterday--uneventful.

Another perfect night. All our planes again left to hand the boche a few souvenirs. While absent tonight, however, the boche planning a little reprisal paid us a visit. We heard the hum of a motor distinctly different, then all lights went out. Suddenly the noise of the motor ceased & we knew he was coasting somewhere above us. All the Frenchmen around the plane scurried to protecting trenches & *cave voûtés*.

Several reports followed each other in quick succession all around us, luckily none were close enough to hit any of the gang. Our machine guns barked out but to no avail for he continued to drop bombs. Two men were wounded about 1000 ft from us but not seriously & the damage was slight. Throughout this bombardment, none of our returning aviators were allowed to land so when the boche left & the field was lighted they land-ed in quick succession.

May 27, En Repos

At 8:30 a.m. this escadrille of bomb dropping airmen was deco-rated by the General of the army for their efficient and brave work. The ceremony took place on the aviation field before all of their aeroplanes, which were lined up, in military order. A band played the Marseilles and a company of French soldiers stood at attention while the general made his speech, decorated the men, & kissed them on each cheek. In the meantime two Spads (fighting planes) did stunts such as loops, dives, and tail-spins above us. The whole effect was most impressive.

The boche flew over again tonight but did little to this section.

May 28, En Repos

Roughe Foster & I took a long walk, assisted by a pickup by a truck this a.m. We went through the forests near Verdun where great numbers of troops are concentrated. Artillery shells, ammu-nition, and supplies are stored in houses and sheds painted with a protective coloring which renders them almost invisible at but a short distance. Even the wagons are painted in this manner. Barbed wire entanglements surround the whole

May 29, En Repos

The Cooks tour continued this morning. We passed a large stone quarry, which is now being worked by a large number of convicts guarded by Arabs wearing bright red turbans. They have been imported for the war from the French Colonies. There are also a large number of other Asiatics working on the road. A great many have jet-black teeth colored in some religious rite. They were brought over originally to fight but they make very poor soldiers & prefer to break stone on the roads.

May 30, En Repos

Clothes over to the spring where I spent the morning doing the wash woman act. The water is very cold and we rub our clothes with a stiff brush after covering them well with soap. This method altho primitive and hard on the garments is universally practiced around here in any nearby brook or spring. The people in the provinces of France are very backward & have none of the little luxuries we are accustomed to in the states. In fact this country seems like another age or a different world.

May 31, En Repose

We walked over to a nearby hill where we inspected a French 75 antiaircraft gun. The presence of a boche is detected by a delicate sounding instrument that will show the vibrations caused by his motors exhaust long before he is in sight. These instruments are so efficient that the number of machines, their type and distance can be detected before they cross the lines. The boche, of course, are able to do the same.

This battery is also equipped with very powerful telescopic glasses and complicated range finding apparatus the operation & principle of which I am not familiar.

June 1, 1917

Still we wait around with practically nothing to do but walk around the country and kick. The French army is, I am afraid, in very sore straits, and most content to carry on this monotonous procrastinating sitting around. An occasional air raid, a local throwing of grenades and perhaps a small unimportant night attack seems to be the only diversion. I am afraid it is up to the English and the old U.S. to do the work. The French are about all in.

June 2, En Repose

The weather of the last few weeks has been perfect. Sunshine, a temperature not to warm to be lethargic and the nights cool enough to require three blankets. The surrounding country is hilly and covered with patches of forest thru which wind innumerable paths barely discernable yet easily traversed. We took a long walk thru these woods today and except for the occasional rumble of a distant battery, we would have imagined ourselves in a forest of Northern Wisconsin. Such thoughts, however, were quickly dispelled when we stumbled over a small mound surmounted by a wooden cross on which a French soldier's hat was tacked. This grave was already overgrown with weeds and was probably dug during the retreat of the fall of 1914.

We leave for Jubécourt tomorrow.

June 3, Front, Jubécourt

Arose at 6:00 packed the tents and other paraphernalia and left for Jubécourt. Arrived in this town & settled by noon. We pitched our tents on the side of a hill & lined up our cars in the valley below. The town is about 100 yards below us. It is typical of the villages in this province. It has about 1000 inhabitants. The buildings are of stone and a small creek runs along one side of it. This creek like most others is sluggish & dirty. There is a water-fall however that affords a good place to bathe. There are also a few stands at which we can wash our clothes. We are, I think, to be more comfortable here than at Vadelaincourt as our environ-ment seems to be more clean & healthful. Johhny, Byron, Porritt, & I left for our first post at Récicourt.

June 4, Front, Récicourt

We arrived at Récicourt in the evening parked our cars in a tum-ble down stable & slept on our stretchers in a nearby house which had been completely riddled. It is very dirty & the rats are quite plentiful. We slept well however, until the early hours of morning when we were awakened by the report of a battery so close that the entire bldg. shook. On looking out we saw that shrapnel was breaking around a boche plane not 200 meters above us.

This town has been completely riddled. First it was bombarded & taken by the Germans, then bombarded & retaken by the French about a year ago. As a consequence there is not a whole house standing. The church was hit by a boche 320 that carried away one half of it. The other half is still used for summer when it is not raining. We are forced to get under cover when we hear the blow of a bugle, which means a hostile plane is approaching. The reason for this is that if the boche know a number of soldiers are in the village they will shell it as it is within easy range. This would be a calamity as the General is now quartered in the town.

June 5, Front, Jubécourt

The breakfast bell rang this a.m. as usual & we after fooling around a bit enter the dining room. We, meaning Johnnie, Harris & I. During breakfast Hathaway our *sous-chef,* who has become a little efficacious, announced that the Little Birds Quartet could wash the White, namely Livingston, Harris, & Conover. We immediately got sore & told Hathaway to go to hell as politely as possible. It seems that while absent at our post it had been announced that all 5 minutes late for breakfast would have to work a car. Well, things were finally smoothed over & we did not work the White. However, relations are still a bit strained.

Went swimming in the river near the town of Rarécourt about 3 kms from here. The water in the swimming hole is about 15 ft in depth & an old house stands on the bank. A window ledge at the second story makes a great diving stand. It sure is a welcome place, particularly at present. We are having very hot weather.

June 6, Front

I washed my clothes in the brook this a.m. Cannot say I am in love with that kind of work. Played baseball with section 15 this aft & we had a good time. Great gang in 15. We played in a soccer field near the village of Dombasle. Our audience was a bunch of poilus & three old Englishmen who are serving in a voluntary ambulance section. They are sinuous, rawboned, wrinkled old fellows too old for regular service. One has ridden the range in Texas for 17 years.

On the way back to our cantonment we were stopped by a stocky *poilu* who asked if we were Americans on receiving an affirmative he jumped up & down with joy said he had lived in San Francisco for 5 yrs. & was going back there right after the war & stay there for good.

June 7, Front

Johnnie & I relieved post 2 which is located up in the woods on the lines at 2 p.m. Shortly after this we carried an *assis* to Récicourt We then returned ate with the *poilus* watched the mule trains of ammunition go by & listened to the guns shoot around us. We finally turned in about eleven o'clock. Shortly after midnight, I was awakened by a booming and crashing that nearly shook me off my stretcher & found that every gun and battery had cut loose. The rattle of the machine guns from this time on was almost incessant for an hour.

At 2:30 a.m. I was again awakened. This time by the Lieut. of the post. A *brancardier* jumped up on the seat beside me and we started out thru the winding narrow roads of the woods on an emergency call to the trenches. A quarter moon standing a bit above the horizon gave us a little light on the open spaces but left us practically blinded behind the trees. The result was that the *brancardier* lost his sense of direction. We got on the wrong road, and found a felled tree blocking our path. Finally cleared this only to run into a shell hole from which we could not extricate ourselves without aid which required about 30 minutes to summon. In the meantime, we were entertained by the bursting of shells & the early morning cuckoo. Finally got on the right road and reached the post where we picked up a *coucher* in pretty bad shape & rushed him to the hospital.

June 9, Front

On call duty at Jubécourt today but nothing out of the ordinary happened.

There is a rumor afoot that Pershing together with his staff has arrived in France. Another rumor has it that 9000 men are also in France. The authenticity of these reports is always very hard to determine.

Last night about 15 of us went down to the épicerie which is also a mill and hay barn. We all sat around an old table, perched on boxes and benches drinking French beer which was served by a very pretty little French girl. On one side was a hay loft & the mill sluice on the other. A smoky lantern gave us our light. You could not have imagined a more weird environment. As I have contended before it isn't the place but the crowd that counts.

June 10, Front

Sunday. Washed my car in the creek this a.m. Walked over to Rarécourt where Section 16 is located with Coulter, Johnnie, & Bigelow & had a swim in the ole pool. Johnnie & I dived off the top of a house at the edge of the creek and startled the natives.

There is some internal dissention in the section at present. We appointed Coulter to ask some questions as to why we were saving money on car allowance for grub. Why the officers received better food than we? Etc. The result was that they received these questions in bad part, got mad, & are now hostile. Guess it will blow over, however, in time.

June 11, Front

On duty at Récicourt today little activity in our line however. I also had my knee dressed in the infirmary & found it to be quite badly infected. Hurt it sliding bases in our baseball game but as it was only skinned I thought no more about it. It seems that the greatest of precautions are necessary as conditions are most unsanitary & they have had a great deal of trouble with tetanus. All wounds no matter how light have to be thoroughly cleansed & disinfected. Glad I learned this when I did.

I have been conversing with one of the French soldiers at this post who has served two years in the trenches. He finally contracted malaria in Salonika and very nearly died. He is not particularly strong now and is occupied in less active work. He tells of experiences in sectors where the boche & French exchanged cigarettes & almost slept together. Then of other times when he was under continual bombardment for days and nights. He is now heartily sick of the war and is praying that it will be over very soon.

Front, June 12

I forgot to mention that our old French Lieutenant who was most undesirable has been taken from us & we now have a new one who seems to be very fine & is of the nobility. The crowd at Jubécourt celebrated this occasion with *beaucoup* de la champagne, speeches & good cheer. In order that we who were so unfortunate as to be at post might also be in on it, he came out with the staff car & brought us champagne, *petite beurre*, chocolate & read his speech which was very good considering his slight knowledge of English.

June 13, Front

Byron Harris had a most difficult time this a.m. He deliberately slept thru breakfast, then to avoid the penalty which is working a car, he claimed that he was sick. We all hooted him & are going to have Roughe Foster play doctor this p.m. Roughe's first patient died. We hope he is more successful this time. Harris. altho a good man with the bull, is beginning to weaken under the pressure of kidding from all sides.

Steve Lewis who was on duty at Post #2 last night walked out into the first line trenches to see the sights. He became so interested that he walked on past our division & into the territory defended by men who were unfamiliar with the American Ambulance Uniform. Suddenly a boche star shell shot up & he was spotted by four or five *poilus* who yelled boche & tackled him from all sides. He had the devil of a time explaining who & what he was & at noon the following day was brought down to us under a heavy guard. Mighty lucky for him that he was not shot.

June 14, Front

Johnnie, the lucky devil has left for Paris to have a false tooth put in his face which has suffered from the contact of bread crust which is about as hard to chew as some friendly rock. He will have an opportunity to get the dope on our entering the aviation & here's hoping.

June 15, Front

Talk about your section gangs! We showed them all up this a.m. when we quarried, cracked & hauled rock. We now have a road leading to the main highway that will make it unnecessary to pull our cars out of the muck in wet weather. After this we all stripped & dived in under the waterfall which altho dirty as hell is cool & refreshing.

At 4 p.m. Heywood & I relieved Post #2, which I have described before. We have encountered a new shift, which comes on every 8 days. The longer we stayed with them the better we liked them. At dinner, there were 12 of us, 11 *poilus* & the Lieut. who was formerly a pharmacist in Paris. Everyone acted natural & we had a most enjoyable time. A Frenchman knows how to enjoy himself & will always meet you more than half way. There is no artificiality as there is in the U.S. and they are all like a gang of kids. One fellow played the mouth organ & several sang. The music was greatly broken up by the discharge of the batteries around us but was nevertheless enjoyed by all. After dinner we watched a nearby battery of 120's shoot & listened to the whistle & boom of the arriving shells.

Front June 16, 1917

Turned in about 10 p.m. but was awakened at midnight by a tremendous bombardment of our artillery. This lasted about 30 minutes when it suddenly silenced & we heard the *poilus* in the trenches yell as they threw hand grenades & shot *torpies.* Meanwhile the northern horizon was well lighted by French & boche star shells. I had scarcely fallen asleep again when our Lieut. came over & routed me out. He informed me that I was to drive out to R1 a post on the eastern part of the line, so I pulled on my shoes climbed into the fliver & drove up the winding road without lights. It was 2:00 a.m. when we reached our destination & got one fellow who was severely wounded in the legs, arm & chest. He was hit by a *torpi.* Three other men but slightly wounded completed the load & we pulled into the hospital at Ville sur Cousances at daybreak.

June 17, Front

The morning was most beautiful & a severe contrast to the freshly mangled men who were being brought into the hospital. War is sure enough hell where it has to destroy the human body in such a terrible manner. My ambulance is sprinkled with blood & the stretchers in the hospitals are red with it. The sufferers seem to complain the least & are sure enough men.

Shorty, Byron & I went out in Byron's fliver, which has been on the rim of late to try it out. We passed thru a most beautiful & picturesque country. Villages half & wholly shot to pieces nestled in valleys or stood out on the top of the wooded hills. We drove 20 kilometers to Ste-Menehould & passed thru some of the most beautiful country of the Argonne. We met Brownie at a station 4 kms. out of the city & took him in with us. Here we met a fellow from Sect 13 also from Chicago.

June 18, Front

We threw a little party & said good bye to Brownie who expects to go to Salonika. Brownie is one fine boy. On returning home, we found that we had broken several military laws by joy riding out of the cantonment & were liable to some terrible punishment. Shorty O'Brien who is rather Irish & dissatisfied got mad altho he was really in the wrong. He left for Paris this a.m. Byron & I are off our cars & in the cantonment for a wk. It was easily worth it 'tho as we must have a bit of change & excitement.

Today we went over to Dombasle & played Sect 15 baseball. Of course, this is *défendu* for me but they said that they needed me to pick the team & catch. I, of course, had to put Harris on the team so he could come over too.

June 19, Front

The days are very much like one another, the fighting is not heavy, we carry a few *blessés* each evening, and spend the remainder of the time arguing about war, politics, women and every other interesting subject on God's green earth.

General Pershing has arrived in Paris with his staff. He represents the first official U.S. forces in France. He was given a most royal welcome and a great deal of stress is laid on his early arrival.

The French soldier is very very sick of this war, his morale is bad, he has born the brunt of this terrible fighting for three years therefore the news of the entrance of the U.S. into the game is dwelt strongly on by the officials who grasp eagerly at every opportunity to cheer their men. I think that the U.S. will have all

WWI Events Second Half of 1917

1917

July   Led by Kerensky Russians begin offensive against Germans in Gallicia. King Constantine of Greece abdicates. Russians retreat along a 155 mile front. Third battle of Ypres begins: French-British troops penetrate along a 20 mile line.

Aug.   Pope Benedict XV pleads for a no annexation, no idemnity peace. (Four weeks later President Wilson rejects peace plea.) China declares war on Germany and Austria-Hungary.

Sept.   Pershing establishes general HQ at Chaumont. Riga captured by Germans. British capture Turkish Mesopotamian army.

Oct.   US enacts War Revenue Act--includes graduated income tax. American troops in trench warfare for first time in France. Austro-German offensive breaks Italian front at Caproetta.

Nov.   First American casualties on Western Front. Germans abandon Chemin des Dames. Canadians capture Passschendaele. Bolsheviks seize Petrograd. Lenin succeeds Kerensky. Clemenceau becomes Premier of France.

Meuse Region Diary Locales

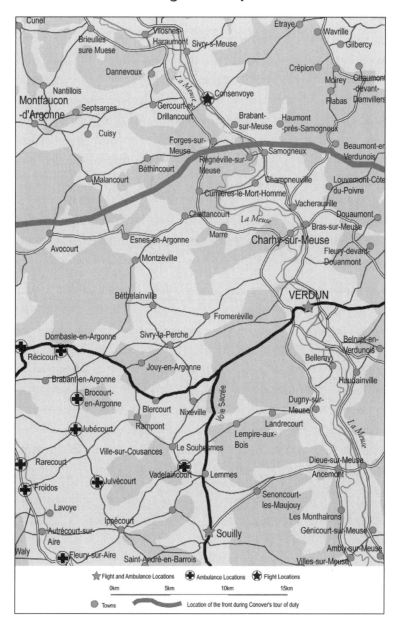

the fighting she wishes before this war is over. France is about worn out, Russia is demoralized and torn with internal strife, the Italians are fair fighters but are not what might be determined aggressive. This leaves England as Belgium has long since been wiped out. England at present is making a mighty good showing. Her army has reached its most efficient stage and she is in the battle with characteristic tenacity. However thru her many mistakes and owing to her first state of unpreparedness she has lost a great many men. She is also suffering heavily from losses at sea caused by the submarine, which is becoming more and more serious. There is no doubt but that she would have been forced to accept most unfavorable terms of peace but for our entrance.

A great deal of stress is now being laid on the aeroplane. Great Britain now claims to be superior to the boche in this department. Her airmen are accomplishing feats hitherto unknown such as diving down on infantry & peppering them full of machine gun holes. Now if aeroplanes can be manufactured in sufficient quantities to keep boche out of the air we can blind them & direct our fire in this way. I believe we can secure ultimate victory. We should, however, stop the submarine. In this weapon lies Germany's greatest hope and one that is far from unfounded.

About the other things, Harris & I are still in the cantonment. Therefore this evening we sneaked over to town & went into the *épicerie*. Here we met two fellows from #16 and threw quite a party. About midnight we sneaked over & got my ambulance out & took these fellows home a distance of about 4 kilometers. We sneaked in without lights in order to avoid detection & nearly ran over an embankment. If this is found out it means yours truly exiting out of the Amer. Ambulance. Funny how taking a chance on things is so enjoyable.

June 23, Front

Johnny, Roughe, Killer & I on duty at Récicourt. Learned that there is to be an attack in a few days. Hope to gawd we will be in it.

Had a shave & haircut in the *coiffeurs* which is located in a shell ridden house one room of which is still intact. The barber is a man who plied his trade before the war in a city in Southern France. He is a little fellow & like all Frenchmen sociable & congenial. This room is also occupied by the tailor of the division sort of a queer combination. The walls are plastered with pictures of women in all kinds of gay & immodest costumes. Frenchmen always collect these pictures & place them in most conspicuous positions. This in my opinion is a very foolish thing to do owing to the scarcity of the opposite sex in the theatre of war & their absence should not be impressed on you if you wish to retain a semblance of mental content.

June 24, Front

Returned from Récicourt after having seen a group of men making an extension to the railroad, which is to carry a 52-centimeter to its mooring. The work is very cleverly concealed by piles of bush & green canvas, which renders the whole thing almost undistinguishable. The French excel all others in this sort of hiding and protective coloration. Their wagons look like some futurists' canvas and are daubed in a seemingly crazy & fantastic manner. The result is, however, that you can approach to a surprising nearness without suspecting their presence.

We heard this evening that there are American soldiers at Vadelaincourt. The report was later proved false. Had a game of soccer with the *poilu* this p.m. & beat them 5-0. A great crowd of soldiers looked on to & proved to be most enthusiastic spectators. We ended up by singing Marquinta & Blondel much to their delight. The French never sing together so any quartet work no matter how poor appeals to them.

June 25, Front

Took the bike this a.m. and rode over to Vadelaincourt, stopped at several towns in search of a glass of beer, but was unable to find same. They have plenty of that damned wine but I can't seem to cultivate a taste for it. Also conversed with several of the country girls & learned that all Americans were rich and chauntie. To be an American in this country at present is to be very popular. I broke the saddle on my bike when returning & was picked up by an English Red Cross Ambulance & given a ride to Ville-sur-Cousances.

Johnny & I went on duty at Post #8 this p.m. but things were unusually quiet.

We walked over to a concealed battery of 255's. The location was shown to us by an obliging Frenchman. These guns are very cleverly concealed & can certainly give a nasty punch. It rained in the evening some were forced to sleep in the underground *abri*. We of course wanted the door open for air & the Frenchmen wanted it closed. We finally won out. Our sleep was terribly broken into by the squealing, moving rats which infest the place by the hundreds. They are half famished & make you a bit nervous when they scamper around & even over you. Your imagination of course conjures up pictures of them eating you after you fall asleep.

June 26, Front

The boche are sending in quite a number of shells this a.m. They remind you of an approaching streetcar as they hum in. We walked down within sight of the boche but they refused to shoot at us for some unknown reason. We passed a grave of a Frenchman, evidently dug where he fell. His helmet was placed on it & contained two clean bullet holes proving conclusively why he lies here. As I write this, the boche shells are intermittently whistling by.

June 27, Front

We were relieved at 4:00 p.m. & carried 4 *blessés* to the hospital at Ville. On arriving at our camp, we found the boys all dressed for a soccer game waiting for us. We immediately changed our clothes & all went down to the field, which was blue with men in uniform. An entire regiment together with their officers & a band had turned out to see us play the best team they could find in the surrounding country. The band played Stars & Stripes Forever as we came on the field & it sure did sound good. Reminded me of the good old football games at home. As the game progressed, we found that our opponents were in for blood & had determined to beat us at all costs. Even the officials favored them in their decisions. This of course made us mad & the game became very rough much to the delight of the *poilus* looking on. For a long time the score stood 2-2 & it was "anybody's game" then we scored another goal in the last ten minutes of play & immediately stood on the defensive. Final score 3-2 our favor. After the game, we treated our opponents to champagne, which relieved the tension considerably.

June 28, Front

Maurice our friend the *chausseur* stopped in & took lunch with us on his way back to his company from his *permission*. He is a mighty fine fellow & it will be a shame if he is shot up in this attack.

At 6:00 p.m. a boche observation balloon was sighted by us much closer than usual & we all went out to have a look. In a few minutes a plane appeared above us and two French Spads engaged him diving and maneuvering, shooting their machine guns the while. Suddenly there was a shriek followed by an explosion & a geyser of mud, rocks, & debris flew in the air 1000 yards from us on the hill. The soldiers who were passing thru the village on the way to the front halted & we saw four more boche planes come in sight. The French Spads disappeared. Another shriek & we all flattened out on the ground. A shell burst about 1000 feet from us.

We then realized that we were not being bombed by the aeroplanes but that we were being fired at by the boche guns 20 miles

away. Their fire was being observed & guided by this big aeroplane above us, The four others were fighters & were protecting
it. Two & a half minutes later a shell plumped in the center of
the road in the middle of the village and killed & wounded some
twenty soldiers. Hiis had started up this road a minute before &
from where we were seemed to have received its full benefit.
Byron & I ran into the town & found he had escaped whole
skinned and already had his car filled with wounded.

I ran back, got my car & returned to a spot which was covered
with wounded & wildly gesticulating Frenchmen. We loaded
one man in & were about to get another when another shriek,
we flattened out & were covered with mud thrown by an *arrivé*
not over 100 feet away. I carried two full loads to the hospital at
Ville & one shell-crazed Frenchman, in spite of my efforts to
push him off, stuck to my car for 2 trips. Hathaway also carried
two loads & Hiis finished up the job.

So on my return a third time we had completely evacuated the
wounded & took refuge behind a house with some *poilus.* I had
been in this position about 30 seconds when the next building
went up in smoke, bricks etc. tumbling about us. On returning
we found our entire kitchen force had scattered & we were
forced to eat scrambled instead of fried eggs, as was originally
planned for our cooks had refused to remain steady. I sure will
hand it to the boche.

July 1, Front

The last few days have been the most busy I have ever spent. The
boche directly after shelling Jubécourt revisited their attention to

the vicinity of the lines, and, after a barrage & heavy bombardment, took some of our first line trenches. We made our headquarters at Récicourt & worked from there to the posts trying to
keep four cars at P2. I had several most exciting experiences &
one narrow escape. On the road to P2 there is one stretch completely open. The boche found this range & were dropping in
shells every 4 minutes. In my approach I saw one explode & fig-
ured I could get by before the next one landed. I did not, however, take the hill into consideration & found myself slowly
climbing it in first speed when there was a shriek, something
flew by my head & seemed to almost hit it. The side of the road
directly behind me was blown high into the air & I was covered
with falling debris.

On advancing further, I ran into a volley of what seemed to be
white smoke & my eyes and throat began to burn. This was my
first experience in gas & I had some difficulty in adjusting my
mask. I then came upon a company of soldiers all wearing
masks. They were a most uncanny sight in the twilight. From
here up to the posts it simply rained shells & the din was terrific.
A French plane flew above us dodging shrapnel & guiding the
fire of our guns which were working overtime. A boche plane
was doing the same. I had an uncomfortable feeling that he was
watching my progress. This deafening fire continued about three
hours. A mighty serious & solemn crowd of fellows worked
through it. Wounded *poilus* walked, limped, & were carried into
post depending upon the character of their wounds. We all evacuated them as fast as we could to the hospital at Ville & returned
wide open.

Needless to say none of us slept & no one expressed the desire to do the same. About three in the morning, the French attacked & a hot hand grenade battle raged. They finally regained their lost trenches & dug themselves in. You certainly have to admire these men in the trenches & can only appreciate the terrible work that they do by actually seeing it. These fellows are <u>real</u> men. Three years fighting these damned Prussians who have been preparing for forty. Three years & they still go in without hesitation to what is death or what seems worse than death to come out maimed & crippled. They are naturally a sociable & peace loving people & to see what the huns have done & knowingly planned makes one consider them as I would a snake. Death is altogether too sweet a thing and too light a punishment for all of them. I can realize for the first time in my life what it means to hate.

July 4, Front - Independence Day

Off today. Decorated the tent with American flags & threw Porritt, who has been accrediting England with too much, into the creek. Had a four-course dinner with plenty of champagne & all went well over to Rarécourt when Section 16 threw a party. Here the general said complimentary things about us. The military band played our national songs, & the drinks were also plentiful. Trust the French for that. Arrived home in a most sociable & enthusiastic frame of mind. After dinner, we held several boxing matches with the Frenchmen while a whole regiment looked on. Overstreet officiated it. Certainly was funny.

July 5, Front

Had a hot soccer game with the 87th--final score 0-0. These fellows are quite young and are sure full of pep. They are very much interested in baseball and have several sore fingers as a consequence. They do not know how to catch a ball & throw very much like a girl. The Frenchman is much more handy with his feet than with his hands.

The arrival of the 87th in Jubécourt has resulted in the acquaintance of a young, clean-cut, almost effeminate, French top sergeant who speaks English quite well. Before the war, he was a jeweler in London. He by nature is the last man you would pick to go into the trenches. He is very sociable & friendly dislikes contests which involve animosity and to use his own words when describing his coming upon three Germans in an attack, "I would have liked to have made friends with them, but I had to kill them with my revolver." This fellow in spite of his natural aversion for war has been in it since the battle of the Marne & has been wounded only once. He has gone in with 200 and come out with 20; has lain in a shell hole biting the ground beneath him for three days while a German machine gun peppered bullets into his knapsack on his back. He relates these experiences quite modestly and in a matter of fact way that carries conviction without bravado. He has undoubtedly been very lucky.

In describing the methods of attack on the trenches, he spoke of the three waves. They are I think quite interesting. The first wave attacks with bombers and machine guns. The bombers also carry short handled picks and shovels strapped to them with which they dig themselves in upon taking a trench. The machine operator plays his instrument upon the retreating boche. The second wave follows the first very closely & is made up of riflemen who watch for any attempted counter attacks. The third wave is made up of men who are known as the cleaners. They follow up with knives & grenades and clean out all the Germans who may be lying in the territory just taken either hiding or wounded. The first wave of course, throws gas bombs into all likely looking holes but the third wave cleans this work up very thoroughly. Prisoners are very rarely taken in such an action because of the necessity of sending men back with them and of their probable treachery. Death is more efficient. Prisoners are only taken in order to get information in case of a large cul de sac.

July 9, Front

Things about the same as usual. Went to the dentist this noon. Army dentists care nothing about their patients feelings but work in the fastest possible manner. I have been hurt before in the dental chair but never so thoroughly and efficiently. Rained practically all day.

Our Ambulance Service Inspector General, A. Piatt Andrew and Major Church, a weak looking U.S.officer, visited us this afternoon. The latter had nothing to say other than to remark about his particular distaste and aversion for shells. Don't blame him much, but I do not think such a sentiment should be expressed by a man of his station to us who see something of them. Bad example. Impression of said major very poor.

GROUP OF AMERICAN AMBULANCE DRIVERS ON THE FRENCH FRONT

July 10, Front

Arose early this a.m. to see machine gun practice of the 87th which expects to leave tonight for Hill 304. These guns are able to shoot 800 times a minute & are the most feared by the soldiers. The officer in charge showed us the guns and allowed us to shoot one. I believe that this instrument is the most efficient death-dealing weapon in the war and its tack-tack-tack has stopped many a boche attack.

HAVING A SPECIAL HOLIDAY AND CELEBRATION, FOR WHICH THE FRENCH COMMANDER IN THAT SECTOR CONTRIBUTED A CASE OF CHAMPAGNE
In the Group Are: "Jack" Platt, B. Bowie, J. MacDonnell, "Kit" Carson, Evanston, Ill.; Lieutenant Delibaule, J. F. Brown, Boston; Cathaway, Prof. Fletcher, Rose Chicago; Robert Meecham, Cleveland; William Agar, New York City; Grant, Blatchford Downing, Kansas City, Mo.; Lewis, Madison, Wis.; John Livingston, Chicago Wilberforce Taylor, Hubbards Grove, Ill.; Paul Welcher, Cleveland; Conover, Albert Gilmore, Madison Wis.; "Red" Woodhouse, George Shaw, "Jack" Moore, California; Paul Lovett, Boston; Le Moyne Sargent, Joseph Keyes, Concord, N

July 11, Front

Things here running smoothly outside of the fact that I have a bum tooth and visited one division dentist who has the Spanish

Inquisition beaten to a stand still. The art of dentistry is not as well developed in France as in the U.S. They know nothing of gold work and their principal remedy is to pull.

I received $22.85 from Butts Myers. Accident insurance I never expected to get. Johnny, Harris, Foster, Smith and I had a little party at the Café de la Mill Stream as a result. Hurée came in later & we gave him some send off. He expects to go to hill 304 with his division to help take back 2 lines of French trenches & to take one of the boche. Hope he pulls thru all right.

July 12, Front

Went out to post this noon and altho we carried a few gas victims things were pretty quiet. Slept at Récicourt in my clothes of course & had one blanket. Nevertheless, I was mighty cold. About 3:00 a.m. in this country it gets very cold no matter how hot the preceding day. This is due to a very heavy mist, which falls nightly, and to the high altitude.

July 13, Front

The boche shelled us twice in Récicourt and we all had a great time excepting Porry who remained in the deepest part of the *abris*, watching the shells come in. They tried to hit the railroad tracks and altho they came mighty close to it, several times they did not score a hit.

Returned to Jubécourt for dinner. After dinner the band struck up the Retreat & 2000 soldiers marched behind it to the strains of the national airs. Star shells and trench lights shot about & the whole crowd sang, yelled and danced around like a bunch of college men after a game. We of course got into it and had the time of our lives. This demonstration takes place but once a yr. before the big holiday and is the most impressive I have yet seen.

July 14, Front

Today is the big national holiday of France. It is in commemoration of the destruction of the Bastille & each soldier is given a cigar, an extra quantity of *pinard*, and a quarter of a bottle of champagne.

We were awakened at 6:30 a.m. by the 87th Division Band playing the Star Spangled Banner in front of our tent. This is considered a very great honor & is accorded only to generals and celebrities, consequently we feel rather conceited at the present time.

Had a game of soccer at 4:00 p.m. The band was present & a great crowd of soldiers. Neither side was able to score throughout the game.

Maurice and his friend the *chasseur* came over for dinner and spent the night with us. They are a great pair & men any nation can be well proud of. Maurice is 27, athletic, and full of pep. He is married & has one child. Before the war, he held a position with the French Stock Exchange & he declares he will return to it immediately after the war. In his own words he is a "patriot not a military man." He is fighting for love of his country rather than for personal glory. He has distinguished himself to such an extent by bravery that he has been decorated with the *Croix de Guerre* with two stars. As a result of this service he has been appointed sergeant major & now takes care of organization and detail work behind the lines. This promotion did not please him, however, for he preferred to remain in the trenches with his comrades. The officials wanted to promote him to the next higher rank only a few days ago & he flatly refused knowing full well that if he accepted he could no longer remain on intimate terms with his friends.

July 15, Front

Went to Récicourt today but things were very quiet in our line. A great deal of traffic passed by throughout the night, however, composed mostly of ammunition and men. An attack is to be made tomorrow morning if the present rumors are correct.

July 16, Front

The boche artillery is much more active than usual & the road to Julvécourt which Roughe Foster & I drove over on the way to the dentist was quite heavily shelled. The Norton Hangers section of American Ambulance men now at Brocourt retreated valiantly. And we were forced to carry our *blessés* through their territory.

Returned to P2 this aft (where I am now) our batteries are quite active all about me. One bunch of 75's fires directly over our heads and almost deafens us at each explosion. A big attack is to be made early tomorrow morning & our artillery is increasing in activity.

July 17, Front

Craig, a young fellow in Sect II located 2 kilometers from here died today as a result of being hit by a shell. His brother is in the same section--mighty tough alright.

The French made a most successful attack this a.m. due to perfect artillery prep encountered little resistance. They advanced 900 meters, took 4 lines of trenches & some 500 prisoners. The artillery fire had left the boche without food for 4 days & the French advance was only stopped by their own barrage.

We were kept very busy and carried boche *blessés* as well as French. A couple of the boche were about 15 years old and cried & asked for their mothers, The *brancardiers* treated them very well & gave them something to eat & drink.

July 18, Front

Several counter attacks were made by the enemy today but all were successfully repulsed by the French who would leap out of their trenches and demolish them with grenades. Our artillery wiped out some 4000 men in one of their attacks. We now hold the top of Hill 304.

I drove all night & never have I seen such traffic. In one place it took me two hours to go one kilometer. The road was a mass of caissons, ammunition, trucks, horses and men cussing at each other. The night was so dark that you could not see a truck more than ten feet off. Porritt ran off the road & turned bottom side up in the ditch. Luckily his *blessés* were *assis* & in some miraculous manner were not hurt. We all banged into different vehicles &

our cars came out more or less beat up. Star shells were being continually shot up & the artillery kept up a continual fire.

The boche made several more counter attacks all were well repulsed. I had three punctures during the night but no other mishap except a bent fender.

July 20, Front

Hurée, the young Frenchman in the 87th whom we became so well acquainted with was killed in this last attack. His body now lies out in no mans land. This sure is hell and brings this war mighty close to home. It has made the whole bunch mighty blue and brings out the terrible part of this war. A young fellow well educated refined and peace loving slaughtered while in the prime of life. His mother nearly died from worry six months ago. What will happen to her now? This is another sacrifice to German kulture, and to their policy of militarism and world domination.

Learned today that the Lafayette Escadrille has been taken over. We are writing to Dr. Gros to accept our applications at once.

July 21, Front

Went down to the épicerie this p.m. for my laundry. Here I met a French lieutenant who insisted upon buying us much champagne. He has just come from Ste. Jouan where he says there are fifty thousand American soldiers. He took part in the 14th celeb. With them and was sure enthusiastic. He could say "All Right" and "Hey" and was mighty funny.

July 22, Front

Left in evening for a 48-hour *permission* in Paris. Took train filled with soldiers at a little jerk water station & hospital centre, Fleury. This train runs on a narrow gauge & makes a maximum speed of about 20 miles an hour. The evening was perfect & the country beautiful. Arrived in Bar-le-Duc at 9 p.m. grabbed a bite to eat & had our tickets made out. Almost sent back to Fleury on account of our perfect French, which did not seem to be recognizable & the similarity of names but finally made it known that we wanted Paris. Met Cadbury in this city. He had ridden in on his bicycle to meet his sister who is doing Red Cross work. She is to leave for England very soon. Certainly seemed good to see an American girl again.

July 23, Paris

Arrived in a *permissionaires* camp at 5:30 a.m. after trying to sleep in a car full of soldiers. Fooled around here until 8 a.m. then caught the train for Paris. Conversed with several French officers who had seen Pershing & were very favorably impressed with the way he and his staff are taking hold of things.

Hit Paris at 9:00 a.m. and believe me it looked good. Three months away from civilization makes this city seem like a paradise.

Spent the rest of the day riding in taxicabs, strolling down the boulevard and seeing the sights. A fellow sure does go wild when he gets back on leave. Spent the evening at our chateau at Rue Braj. Very large & most enjoyable.

July 24, Paris

Went down to Naval Offices in regard to entrance into the aviation. As usual they know nothing definite, can give you slight
encouragement, and regard you from their lofty and superior
ranks as if they were showing favoritism in talking to you. Believe
me, these fellows will change and experience is sure a dear
teacher.

Met Ray Williams a fellow I knew at Wisconsin. He is serving in
Section 12. We, together with Hath, Cookie, & Smith, went
down to the Olympian & had a great time. This theatre is filled
with girls and they sure are there! Don't believe I will ever be satisfied with the American girls again. They are spoiled beyond
repair.

July 25, Paris

Spent the morning conferring with the Army Aviation and
received a little more satisfaction. They, however, demand proof
that you are a gentleman. This proof must be in the form of letters of recommendation from men who have known you long
enough to swear to your integrity and Christian character. This
is of course well nigh impossible as we have spent all of our time
in the field and have had no opportunity to become acquainted
with men of standing in the community. Again, I state that these
officers are a bunch of damned fools. I will, however, get letters
if I have to bribe people for them.

Spent evening with Cookie Roy same place. Also can state that
Georgette is some girl. Jet black hair — Well I hate to think of the

journey back to the front.

July 26, Paris

Today I moved down to the Hotel de Etats Unis. A man who is half-Italian & half American runs this. Two of the patrons can play the piano & about any other instrument in the world. We had a concert that was sure great & I certainly did enjoy it.

Turned in for the first good sleep since my arrival.

July 27, Paris

Went out to the dentist first thing this a.m. He has come over very recently & wears an ambulance uniform. Like all new men, he wants to appear old. I, therefore, struck up a contract with him that I should be kept over for my teeth & in return give him the old insignia which I don't care a damn about.

Took lunch with a Mr. Hoetsel, friend of Ray's, and it sure was some feed. After lunch bumped into an old man who lived in Fondulac 20 years ago, and has a son out at the front. He has a picture of his son together with Navarre. He invited us to come out to tea.

In evening went to Olympian where we did the usual thing after returning. At about 12 o'clock the sirens began to blow & lights went out warning us of a zeppelin or aeroplane raid. We all beat it for the open square where we could watch developments. Searchlights played about the sky and aeroplanes with small lights on them to distinguish them from the enemy shot about the sky. The boche disappointed us however & after a long wait the crowd dispersed. Instead of hiding in a cellar the people had come out to watch it & were greatly disappointed that nothing happened. This, I think, was a wonderful example of the courageousness of the French people.

I bribed the dentist to let me stay over until Tuesday with a number of souvenirs. Ray Williams & I took Georgette & Valenti out to dinner & had the time of our lives. Best looking women I have ever seen & pep! As I said before I will never again be satisfied with American girls.

July 29, Paris

Ray, Dick Stout & I took a boat up the Seine in p.m. & strolled about the Bois de Boulogne. Most beautiful park filled with amorous couples.

Went down to the Ambassador for tea and ended up at Raymonard for dinner.

In the evening, we went down to the Retonde Café a famous restaurant in the Latin Quarter. Here we met another girl who has made the biggest hit of them all. Her name is Isabelle & she is, to say the least, distinctly French. The three of us bought some wine & went over to her room, which is most interesting. The evening was, to say the least, sociable.

July 30, Paris

Finished up with the dentist today & gave him his last souvenir. Had quite a talk with some Englishmen & Canadians at the Knickerbocker Bar. One Englishman has been in the army since he was fourteen years old and has traveled all over the world. He is one of the famous Indian gunners, only a few of whom are now left. He tells some great tales and is a very interesting and attractive cuss to say the least. He has brought up my opinion of the English a great deal.

July 31, En Route Front

Left for Ste-Menehould this noon & took a first class coach with the officers. From Ste-Menehould we are to drive to Jubécourt where our section is located.

Arrived at 8:00 p.m. & spent our last cent for egg sandwiches & beer. We then learned that our section has moved & is somewhere near Bar-le-Duc. This is pleasant as we are without a *sou* and there is no train until tomorrow morning. Stranded in a foreign country without a cent. Certainly seems funny.

Late in evening, we met Brownie of #19 on his way to Paris. He loaned us 10 francs so we put up in style in a hotel & had breakfast. The bill amounted to 9.5 francs.

August 1, En Route Front

Started for Bar-le-Duc in a.m. Finally arrived there after changing & finally asking an engineer where he was going. Had a cup of coffee & piece of bread for lunch. Broke again. Met some U.S. soldiers in the afternoon, however, & inveigled them into buying us something to eat. Also described conditions at the front & scared them half to death. One said he would not care but that he has a family he wants to see again.

These Frenchmen seem very slow. After finding out where our section was located, they took all afternoon to try to get them on the phone. They finally told us to come around tomorrow and we immediately got mad and bawled them out with great feeling. They ended up by giving us a pass on a train that was to leave for gawd knows where. We went down to the station there ran into some of the boys who had come to see the sights.

August 2, Condé

We are *en repose* at a little town about 20 kilometers from Bar-le-Duc. We have very good quarters & are comfortable. Maurice & the *chausseurs* are located in the next village.

Two more ambulance men have just been killed. Such things are getting to be pretty common now.

This evening I was called out to relieve a car in pain at Ville where six of our cars are helping out the new section. It was raining like the devil, and I had to find my way over unfamiliar roads, but was able to get there by inquiring in every village. The post was a run of about 40 kms.

August 3, Condé

I was called out for a trip at midnight & carried three *couchés* to Fleury. It rained so hard that I was able to keep only one eye open and had to keep on the road more by guess than anything else. We spent two days working here, were finally relieved, and returned again to calm. Four more ambulance men have been wounded. Two of them are not expected to live.

August 4, Condé

Rained all day today and was damp and cold. The cable from New York states that today is the hottest day in history and 128 people have been killed by the heat.

China has declared war on Germany now. She has 400,000,000 men but what good are men without organization in this war?

Maurice & Toto came over this evening & we all walked down to their quarters, drank beer, talked, and listened to Maurice play his violin. We have an opportunity out here of becoming well acquainted with the Frenchmen. This opportunity moreover will not be given to the U.S. boys when they come over.

August 5, Condé

This is Sunday morning because we had bacon, eggs and chocolate instead of the daily coffee & bread for breakfast. Therefore let's all be thankful for Sunday & only hope it will come more often in the future.

We shot our dog Stripes today. He is the first dog we have had to shoot in the last day. Rummy, Sausage, Stars & Stripes are all under the soil, and all have had the same disease. Am afraid Whiskey will also have to be crocked for he has the same malady. Maurice & Frank were over to dinner. Maurice brought his violin & we had a concert also a dance with a girl Johnny found in the village.

August 6, Condé

Played soccer with the Chausseurs this p.m. Maurice hurt his knee pretty badly and as a result is hardly able to walk. We went down to see him after dinner and as usual he furnished us with beer. He certainly is a fine fellow and is one the French nation can be mighty proud of. He can't go to the hospital because of his grade and the way he received his injury.

August 7, Condé

Went to Bar-le-Duc today and met an aviator of the French Army. He was formerly a member of Section I and is a citizen of Cuba. Has been in the game since 1915, and tells some mighty interesting tales.

This evening Johnny & I strolled about the village. It seemed unusually peaceful. A phonograph played in the Foyer de Soldat, and the civilians and soldiers quartered here walked slowly about or laughed and talked in little bunches. The air was hot and moist. A slight breeze was blowing from the south but was noticeable only occasionally. At nine thirty the buglers came out sounded their taps and the crowd gradually dispersed. One group of soldiers which leaves tonight, however, stood at attention and answered to roll call. The southerly breeze had gradually increased in strength until it gained the velocity of a gale. Lightning began to play in the south and an occasional drop of rain spattered against our faces. The streets by this time were completely deserted.

Suddenly two staff cars loomed up in the dusk running without lights. Immediately following these at intervals of seventy-five feet rolled immense *camions* packed with French soldiers on their way to Hill 304 and the lines. Some of these *camions* contained men who were singing, others talked and laughed, others were apparently quarreling and others passed by in silence. All, however, seemed to be oblivious of the fact that most of them would be wounded, some would be killed and the remainder would only come back to return to the same hell of fire, gas, steel, and suffering. They were not oblivious of this fact, however, for practically all of them have been through this very same thing before and know full well that each succeeding attack is more terrible than the last. But why worry about it when worrying does not alter the condition? This is, of course, their logic and the only thing that saves them from losing their minds.

After fully seventy-five of these *camions* had passed there was a great crash of thunder and the storm broke. We immediately ran for our quarters where we could still hear these gigantic vehicles rumble by and an occasional song could be heard from these men on their way up to destruction.

Such things as these, after a man has seen the terrible effect of this fighting, are bound to make him hate war with a loathing indescribable. And what is the good of it? What is gained? You practice, plan, invent, and strive to kill men in the most scientific and dreadful way possible. Then you try to mend those who are only half dead and to make it possible for them to remain on earth so maimed and disfigured that perhaps death would be more welcome.

After these Germans have been beaten; after their Kaiser and military empire is destroyed (if such a thing is ever possible) I will be the most ardent pacifist, the most strenuous peace advocate and contrite military man in this world.

August 12, Condé

Received orders to move up to the front again. It seems we are to do evacuation work as our division is pretty well shot up. We are to have two cars at Ville, 15 at Brocourt, & three on reserve. They are planning a big offensive as soon as the weather permits. At present, however, the trenches are filled with water due to the extraordinarily heavy rains that we have had.

There is a report that the boche have introduced a new gas, the odor of which cannot be detected and the effects are not noticed until 24 hours after exposure. This gas is intensely dangerous and burns your skin as well as your lungs.

We have just had an inspection of masks and instructions as to the proper action to take for this particular variety.

This evening we went down to the corner cave and had a most sociable time assisted by several Frenchmen.

August 13, Condé to Ville

We left Condé in convoy order at 7:00 p.m. and ran up to Ville-sur-Cousances. The country about this village is absolutely filled with men and the roads a mass of traffic. The boche made an attack tonight after a very heavy bombardment. Section 31, which has been taking our post, fell down completely. Two men deserted their cars when caught in gas. One of them had three boches, all of whom were found dead in the morning. If a Frenchman had done this he would have been shot without hesitation. In spite of the fact that these were absolutely green men, I think the same should be done in this case. It is an insult and disgrace to the American people and shows the kind of men who might consider taking up ambulance work with the idea of saving their skins. Five of our cars were finally called upon to clean up the mess.

During this action 150 boche soldiers walked over and gave themselves up. A curious incident occurred. One of these men was formally a waiter in a Paris restaurant & he encountered the proprietor his former employer in the trenches. He was overjoyed to see him and endeavored to shake him by the hand.

August 15, Ville

We are taking care of the transportation work from Brocourt and Ville. Because of the fact that our division has been loaned to several others, we do not have charge of our former post. If, however, #31 falls down again we will replace them.

Our quarters in Ville are terrible due of course to the congestion in the sector. Some twenty-five of us are in a tent that should be occupied by half of that number and our effects are tumbled in one chaotic pile. It rains or rather pours about three times every day & five times every night. As result, the sensation of being dry has long since been forgotten. The roads are a mass of mud & water that flies high in the air when you drive through it. Since moreover our cars are the lightest on the road, we receive more than our share. But as the Frenchman says, *"C'est la guerre."*

August 16, Ville

It is now a matter of only a few days before the big French attack is to be made. The reports say that it will be the last of the year & every effort is being made to make it successful. The French people certainly need cheering up & we are all hoping that it will be a big success. The weather, however, has been against them. The trenches are waist deep with water, and I still have a great respect for the boche organization.

August 17, Ville

We are now running on 24 hour shifts, sleeping every other night. *Blessés* are already numerous, most of them being victims of gas.

August 18, Ville

I have been so busy during this week that I have had no opportunity to write of the transpiring events.

The week was a most unpleasant one. We have been doing only evacuation work due to the fact that our division is still on repose and we were called for emergency work. Our post is a field hospital located at Brocourt, which is some five kilometers behind the lines. From this point we were forced to evacuate all *blessés* brought in by the sections operating at the advance dressing stations. We evacuated to hospitals at Ville, Froidos, Rarécourt, Fleury, Vadelaincourt and Souilly. These towns are located within a radius of thirty to forty kilometers & in each town is a hospital taking care of specialty cases.

August 19, Ville

The roads are crowded with vehicles of all descriptions and are coated with a fine powdery dust that flies in clouds so thick that one is unable to see more than a few feet ahead. We are quartered in a dirty little barrack and are furnished with still more dirty blankets thrown over improvised beds made of mesh wire. On these palatial couches, we snatch an hour or so of sleep whenever a slight let up in the stream of *blessés* allows us. Out of the week's work I was able to obtain two nights of real sleep.

Naturally, these conditions are far from conducive to a satisfied feeling, especially since our meals which consist of coffee for breakfast & some kind of greasy boiled meat with either beans or spaghetti are far from palatable. Therefore, our section is most dissatisfied & crabby. If we were able to get up into the lines where the big show is going on everything would be fine but this matter of hardship & discomfort without a bit of excitement to relieve the monotony is somewhat nerve racking.

August 21, Ville

The French have during this time made two attacks which are the most successful of any since the war began from a point of view of territory gained, prisoners, and losses. About 7000 boche prisoners were taken. A goodly number of guns, Mort Homme & Hill 304 captured, and the boche counterattacks successfully repulsed.

We have seen & talked to a great many German prisoners. They all seem to be of the same caliber. The common soldiers walk in a slow, plodding manner and some appear glad to have been taken prisoners. The officers are arrogant and sneering. They walk with their heads high and are a remarkable type of perfection in militarism.

August 22, Ville

Of course, we have been gathering souvenirs when possible and in connection with this work a humerous incident took place. About a hundred prisoners were marching by under the guard of mounted gendarmes. The usual crowd of soldiers looked on jeering at them and calling them names. I cranked my car & Red Foster jumped in the seat beside me. As I drove along this line Red reached out grabbed a boche cap from the top of a hun's head. He of course objected for going about the world bare headed is not the pleasantest thing to do especially during the chill damp fall nights. However, his objections came too late as we drove by.

August 23, Ville

The evening was perfect. As we drove back and forth, the flashes of the guns & star shells were a wonderful sight. Great searchlights shot their rays far into the sky in search of boche planes & colored rockets flared about signaling our own aeroplanes. Suddenly an unusually bright light appeared about ten kilometers to the west of us. It rapidly increased in size until it lighted a large part of the western horizon. Flashes from the bursting shells of our antiaircraft guns appeared directly above it explaining its cause to us instantly. A number of boche planes had flown over & dropped inflammatory bombs upon the hospital at Vadelaincourt. The destruction was terrible for the poor wounded men lying in beds could not escape. Those who were not killed by the explosions were burned to death. This is another example of the German kultur and has been actually witnessed by me. This conclusively proves in my estimation the truth of stories of this character, which I have heretofore doubted.

August 25, Ville

A great many French planes have been transported to our sector and have operated so thoroughly & successfully that a boche observer has become a rarity. However one appeared about the middle of the afternoon & one of our planes immediately gave chase. The next thing we knew we saw the boche falling in great whirls first rapidly then slowly. It seems that our aviator had killed the pilot & the observer was attempting to right the machine. His efforts, although in vain, served to lighten his fall. He crashed into the branches of a tree & the observer altho hurt was carried away to the hospital with a good chance to recover.

Lufbery of the American escadrille is said to have done the work. This makes his ninth plane & was as beautiful & spectacular a sight as I ever expect to witness.

August 27, Ville

Section 17 running true to form—Several of us while off duty today went down to the Café de la Mill Stream at Jubécourt. Quite a party was held. Johnny, Pete, and I however left early leaving Roughe, Harry Overstreet & Harvey to finish up. In the meantime Cadbury our *sous chef,* who is a snake, saw these fellows and attempted to tell them what to do. The result of course was that he was politely told to go to the nether regions. Then the trouble started. Cadbury told Neftel, Neftel immediately fired them. In the meantime, I found Neftel and did some of the fastest talking I have ever been called upon to execute. Neftel finally relented & things are again o.k.

August 28, Ville

Harris & Bigelow are the next to distinguish themselves. They took a joy ride to Ste-Menehould and, as luck would have it, ran right into the staff car. They were immediately fired and leave for Paris tonight. Harris who is our star baritone will be greatly missed so we all rendered our last ditties. We lined up in front of the car as they left to shoot revolvers as is becoming to a true military farewell.

The feeling between the officers and fellows is now at the breaking point. It is a big question as to whether we will be able to live together for the next two weeks when our time is up. I am sure enough fed up with this ambulance game & am counting the days before we leave.

August 30, Mesnil

We left Ville today and drove to Mesnil-sur-Oger. This little village, about 15 kilometers from Épernay, is in the very heart of the champagne district. It is much richer, is inhabited by a better class of people, & is much more attractive.

We are surrounded by vast fields of grapes, all of which have just ripened, and we have already become sick of them.

Some of the most famous brands of wine in the world are manufactured in this district. Clicquot, Pommerey, Mercui, etc. can be bought for about 5 francs a bottle.

We are quartered in the village school are sleeping in two adjoining classrooms and eating in another. The rooms are lighted by electricity, which is going at all times, and we are plentifully supplied with water from a pump in the front yard.

August 31, Mesnil

We held our farewell banquet this evening and it was a rousing success.

We started out at the *épicerie* and ended up at the Café de la Paix of the village. Each man gave a talk & the singing was wonderful. Love one another and forget all petty differences was the spirit that permeated the entire function and there was no one who did not pronounce the celebration as a most fitting termination of the very famous section seventeen which is soon to be no more. The health of every member, excepting of course that of the deceitful Cadbury, was drunk in the very best champagne not once but many times and we all retired feeling that there has been no other bunch quite as good as ours.

The Mayor of the village upon hearing that we were having our farewell party gave us special permits to carry it out without being hindered by the 9:30 p.m. closing law.

Two full glasses were placed in the center of the table in honor of Harris & Bigelow, who had been forced to go to Paris a bit early, and we showed them our true feelings by solemnly pledging their health from their glasses to the tune of the loving cup at the end of the party.

September 1, Mesnil

Porry, Bill Richards, Harry Overstreet, Kearfoot, left for Paris today. All of these men with the possible exception of Bill will enter some other branch of the service. Everyone is very much up in the air over this question as our time is practically up and an action is necessary. The U.S. Govt. has now taken over the service and is signing up the men who wish to remain in it for the duration of the war.

September 3, Mesnil

I went in to Épernay today to get a bath, but owing to the fact that the war prohibits bathing on Monday I was unsuccessful. We strolled about the town, which is quite pretty and saw several of the wind factories.

The boche occupied this country for only nine days, and luckily did not have time to ravage and demolish it owing to their hasty retreat from Paris. They did, however, help themselves most liberally to the wine. It is claimed that this action, as much as anything else, prevented them from being more successful. The officers and men were drunk in such large numbers that they were unable to execute their necessary orders in anything like an efficient manner.

September 5, Mesnil

Neftel got back today from Paris where he has been getting new men. He has recruited six and is expecting to get more shortly.

September 6, Mesnil

Sold my bed for 20 francs to the Sarge. Everyone is selling his effects at bargain prices and the frenchmen, who love to barter, are in their glory.

September 7, Paris

We all took the train from Épernay at 12:30 p.m. and arrived in Paris about 3:00. I went out to Nuilly hospital and had my teeth looked over preparatory to my examination for the aviation.

In the evening we all went down to the Olympia and saw all of our old friends, among them were Georgette & Valentine, looking just as pretty as ever.

I ran into Dave Annan today and was surely surprised. He has been over with the ambulance for about three months. Also met Ed Hasbrook who has been in Section 28 & is now on his permission. This certainly is a small world after all.

September 8, Paris

Had my physical exam for the aviation this morning and it lasted about two hours. I did everything imaginable from hopping & balancing on one foot with eyes closed to whirling on a stool with goggles on. I passed it successfully and took the mental test right afterward. This test however, was very simple!

Went over to see Isabelle in the afternoon & found her with her family that is down for a visit. She has a younger sister even better looking than herself. Took her out to dinner after having had tea at her home & shaken a Spanish friend from South America.

September 9, Paris

Went to Rue Raynouard this a.m. & met the gang, Neftel among them. He is in to look over new men for his section. This meeting started a party that will go down in history. We stopped in at the Tourelles then ate dinner at the Brasserie Universal. From there we went to the ball game at San Cloud but this proved uninteresting so we took a sea-going hack back to the Café de la Paix. From here we went to the Café de la Sports & from there to the Artistes. This last place was filled with Canadians, Australians, New Zealanders & Scottish Highlanders. We then sang every song we had ever heard. Finally, led by Nefty's friend Georgette, we marched back to the Sports and had dinner. From here, we marched, singing all the time, to the Folies Bergere, which was packed to overflowing & finally ended up in a supreme climax with the representatives of the chorus in a nearby café.

September 10, Paris

The next morning was spent by Johnny & me in preparing to leave for Biarritz for a few days. Byron, Roughe, Big, David Goodman, the Australian who has been all over the world, Johnny, and I took dinner at Pruniere the most famous place for sea foods in Paris. Afterwards Johnny & I took the 8:25 for Biarritz.

September 11, Biarritz

The night on the train was most uncomfortable for although we had first class seats, our compartment was filled and as usual, the Frenchmen closed all windows and doors. We stood it as long as possible but finally when on the point of suffocation we got out.

The ride through southern France is quite pretty and although the land is comparatively flat, there are large stretches of pine forests, which give a beautiful effect.

We arrived in Biarritz around noon and took a sea-going hack to the Carlton Hotel. Here we were lucky enough to secure their last room. We sat down to a most excellent luncheon, tired but happy. The Carlton is one of the best hotels in Biarritz and in spite of such restrictions as meatless days etc., serves as good meals as the best hotel in America. The patrons are a mixed lot, a few English and quite a number of French and Spanish. They are mostly of the nobility and the women are superb.

Biarritz is one of the most fashionable and famous watering places in Europe. It is located upon a most beautiful indented shore and has two very fine bathing beaches. It also has a very nice golf club and some fine tennis courts. Our program while staying here has been as follows: Swim in the morning, and the water is great; Luncheon at one; Afternoons we generally take a trip to one of the places of interest or go up to the country club; Tea at five; Promenade from 7 p.m. until eight; Dinner at 8. After dinner there is the cinema, the opera, or anything else you wish. I have been having the time of my life down here and hate to think of leaving on Saturday but suppose that is the best.

We went down to Bayonne, a little seaport town about seven kilometers from here and one of the most ancient villages of Southern France. It is particularly interesting because of its old fortifications, which are still in a fair state of preservation, and because of a very ancient castle which was at one time the stronghold of the Black Prince and Pedro the cruel. It is *défendu* to go through this castle because of the war and the fact that it is being used for officers headquarters in which valuable papers are being stored. However we walked in, saw the place from top to bottom, walked about the look out & saw many most interesting relics. Just as we had finished a gendarme grabbed us & took us over to the officer in charge of the place. We had a hard time convincing this man that we were not German spies but finally succeeded in doing so.

September 15, Biarritz

Saturday. Both Johnny & I felt very blue at the prospect of leaving this haven. So blue in fact that we decided to defy the powers that be and remain here until Tuesday.

We interviewed Mr. Carter upon this matter & he advised us to stay and have a good time. He even offered to loan us money until I could reimburse him from my account in Paris. He is a very fine man, a patriotic American through and through. He is the kind of man who makes you feel proud to be an American. He has lived in France for about 11 years and is I think rather prominent. He seems to carry a great deal of prestige with him and is a fine mixer and a thorough judge of men. He is moreover, very opinionated as to the duties and qualifications of an

American and is apt to say just what he thinks.

September 16, Biarritz

Sunday. Arose early this a.m. and played tennis at the country club. Surf bathing afterward then we went to a bullfight in the afternoon. The bulls were very bad and two of the Toreadors were quite seriously gouged.

Several South American lads took part in the amateur event and did very well. A Portuguese boy of about 17, who is staying at our hotel, displayed a great deal of nerve and was knocked down twice. Luckily, he was not injured.

September 17, Biarritz

Last night we dined with two Canadians who are spending their furlough here. They are mighty fine chaps and very interesting. They have been over for two years and have been through Vimy Ridge. Went swimming twice today: first at Port Vieux, and in the afternoon in the surf at the Plange. We had the Canadians with us tonight and afterward went to see our friends in the town.

September 18, Biarritz

Spent the morning in the water and it sure was great. We swam out to the big rock, a distance of about half a mile, and dived from its top. The drop is sheer and with an elevation of about thirty feet so the sport was not a bit bad.

We leave for Paris this afternoon and it makes us mighty blue to think about it. However, we've had a great time and I suppose, should not kick.We met the two Canadians at the train and finally managed to get a compartment, which the four of us determined to hold against all comers. This was a rather difficult task for the train was crowded with a great many people standing and our compartment was meant for eight rather than four. We accomplished this feat however by tacking up a sign on the door and holding it against all comers. The sign read as follows:

> La Compartment est reservé
>
> por les officiers des Allies
>
> **VIVE LA FRANCE**

The night was terribly hot & the traveling uncomfortable, but in spite of this fact we enjoyed ourselves immensely.

September 20, Paris

Arrived in Paris in the a.m. Met Roughe Foster and we all went down to the U.S. Aviation offices and took the oath of service. Our time with the Ambulance has now been finished and we are prospective pilots in the U.S. Aviation Service. We are, however, still living and eating at the Ambulance headquarters and will continue to so until we are thrown out bodily. The reason for this is most simple and can be explained in one word–finance. We have lived like millionaires for a couple of weeks. Now we must accept the other extreme and await the next rise.

Now that we are in the Aviation it is necessary for us to report at 8:30 a.m. and remain until 6:00 p.m. Our duties are mostly sitting around but it will take some few days before there will be room for us in the aviation school.

September 21, Paris

Section Seventeen, that is the original seventeen of last March has been scattered and I am afraid will never again be able to get together. It is a big question as to how many and what percentage of them will last through the war. Our men so far have taken the following action. Bill Richards enlisted for the duration with the ambulance. He is the only man in original bunch to do this.

Roger Nutt, being too young for any service, is going home to continue school. L.K. Porritt & Ira Woodhouse have enlisted in the Naval Air Service A.P. Foster, J.W. Livingston, O.R. McMurry, E.T. Hathaway, V. Heywood, D.A. Bigelow, and I are in the U.S. Aviation. F.C. Kearfoot and Harry Overstreet have applied for artillery. L.M Garner has been accepted. Steve Lewis and Hiis are to get into the aviation or artillery. Looks like a pretty good record for A.F.S. Section 17.

September 23, Paris

We are now awaiting our turn to go to Tours. In the meantime, I am assisting in the Medical Department which is examining the men who are applying for admission into the aviation service. It is quite interesting to see the men as physical specimens and to note the various reactions to the tests they are subjected to.

We have been living and eating at the Ambulance Quarters, I am afraid we will not be able to get by with it much longer as there are a great many men trying the same thing we are and they are checking up rather closely upon the men who are no longer in the service. We have fooled them so far, however, by eating with the officers where they assume no man would have the crust to go unless he was directly connected with the service and by sleeping in the chapel at Rue Lesain where Emil guards our beds for which we no longer have a right.. There is nothing like a lack of finances. It makes a man swallow his pride.

We have tried to procure an allowance from the govt. for living expenses but the authorities are up against a stone wall and can do nothing. Therefore, I decided inasmuch as I did not relish the idea of sleeping in dirty beds infested with bugs that I had better wire for finances.

September 25, Paris

We spent the evening in a two-frame hotel and found it comfortable if not gaudy. Have decided to get into a Hotel with a pension however and we move into one on the Ave. Montaigne tomorrow. It is near to our headquarters and very comfortable.

September 26, Paris

Paris is much more lively than last spring and the prices of all things have jumped tremendously. Americans who were an objects of curiosity last March are now disgustingly common and our uniforms excite very little interest. This condition is most discouraging particularly after one has become accustomed to being noticed by everyone.

The music halls and bars are thronged with Canadians and Australians, most of who have not had a permission for twelve to eighteen months. The natural result is that they relax in every sense of the word and things are made rather lively.

September 27, Paris

A man's ideas change a great deal after he has served in the hell at the lines where one life counts for nothing and is flicked out causing no more commotion than the death of a mosquito. He realizes this full well and his actions on leave are only a logical result. For he knows that after a few days respite he must again return to the front with a good chance of not coming out. Then why should he not enjoy himself while on leave to the fullest extent, regardless of the consequences? Why should he not spend all of his money as he may never again be able to use it? This result of the war is, I think, to be felt more deeply after it than most people realize for a man's actions are bound to affect him in later life and habits of living are much more easily made than broken. This result in the social conditions after the war will be a most interesting one. The French customs, habits, and morals will also play a part in this result. I wonder if more of their weaker traits will not be assimilated than the good ones. The women of the streets, different from those in America in many respects, may play a more important part than people imagine.

September 29, Tours

We left for Tours this morning and after four hours on the train we arrived and were taken directly to the camp. Here we saw Hathaway, Foster, McMurry, and Bigelow.

The quarters are very comfortable, the food good, the authorities in charge very lenient and accommodating, and everything seems to point to a most pleasant prospect. To summarize the whole outlook we have just three things to do—Eat, Sleep, and

Fly. Who could ask for anything more agreeable?

September 30, Tours

The life here is becoming more agreeable each day. It is the greatest relief in the world after having lead a life of shiftlessness in the ambulance for six months to have a definite purpose, some end in life, and to feel that you are accomplishing something.

We get up while it is still dark, eat breakfast, and this morning we had roll call in the moonlight. We then go to our respective fields; there being six of us in each class, and start flying at sun rise. The reason for this is that the air is least bumpy in the early morning and late evening.

We eat again at eleven, have two hours off, and drill for about twenty minutes some days. Food again at three, after this flying until dark. Back to a fourth meal at 7:45 p.m. Then we go to the canteen or to Tours & enjoy ourselves. Lights are out at ten.

October 1, Tours

Took my first flight today and sure was crazy about it. I really believe that I enjoy flying more than sailing and that is going some.

October 2, Tours

I had two flights today and a.m. becoming more accustomed to sailing about in the air. The landing, however, is to be difficult, and there is a great thrill when you dive down and see the ground rush suddenly up to meet you. The instructors vary greatly in their methods, and I believe I am very lucky in getting a man who is not afraid. Teaching a man is naturally a ticklish job, but he allowed me to take the controls the second time up. He believes in banking all turns & does not teach us to use the rudder at all. Yesterday while taking Browning up, he signaled for him to bank & Browning banked & climbed at the same time. This is a most dangerous thing to do at a height of 200 meters, & our instructor says he considers himself lucky in being alive at the present moment--an inch more & he would have gone into a wing slip. His name is Lieut. Fere.

October 3, Tours

This morning due to the unsettled weather conditions we did not fly. It cleared up by evening, however, and I got in a ten-minute flight in which I feel I am making progress.

It has been truly said that a man is never satisfied. He makes something his goal and after having reached it, wishes to go on. I set my heart on entering the aviation and spent four months corresponding and arranging for entrance. Now I think of nothing but completing my course successfully, of being brevetted. Then there will be the Nieuport school, which I hope to be able to attend. Having mastered this I will want to make a record at the front and so it goes on to infinity, and I wonder if anyone with ambition has ever been satisfied after reaching his goal or if he wishes to go on. Does a man ever feel satisfied with the results of his efforts even if he outdoes himself and accomplishes things far beyond his expectations?

October 5, Tours

We are unfortunately getting a taste of bad weather, which always accompanies the equinoctial season in France. High winds and intermittent rain are absolutely the worst things possible for flying. Today we were unable to do anything in the flying line, and we spent our time getting settled in our new barracks. McMurry, Foster, Johnnie, & I are fortunate enough to receive officers quarters, and each of us has a private room containing a dresser, bed, work stand, and table. It is a great relief after having spent seven months in the most congested quarters to again get a taste of comfort. Our rooms, which are the simplest possible, seem most elaborate and luxurious.

October 6, Tours

Fifty new men arrived today, filling the school to overflowing. They all have attended the ground school in the States for three months and have been in France only three weeks. They were first sent to Issoudun and allowed to dig latrines and build barracks, as the school in that town has no machines. They term themselves the flying carpenters and are mighty glad to have been sent here where they will have an opportunity to learn to fly. Sheep Alexander who I knew at Madison is with them. They all appear to be very fine fellows. Got in one flight.

October 7, Tours

This is another unfavorable day for flying, and I think I will celebrate by writing home to the folks. Am afraid the news of Codie Cambell's death will not cheer them up to any extent. I hope they do not hear about it.

The weather continues to be unfavorable with high winds and intermittent rain. The chief diversion about camp is conjecturing as to when we will be paid. Practically everyone is broke and it becomes more and more of a problem to keep in smokes. A certain amount of government red tape has to be gone thru before we receive our wages, and the army seems so disorganized that it is impossible to foretell when the powers that be will come across.

October 8, Tours

I have been quite interested in observing the fellows that have joined this service. It is of course reputed as being the most dangerous game and is often termed the suicide club of the U.S. Army. Therefore, I think, inasmuch as the enlistment is voluntary and each man has entered only because he wanted to, that particular attention should be given to the motives of the enlistee. A great many influences such as adventure, romance, pursuit of glory, etc. of course played an important part, but I can not help believing that the greatest influence was patriotism for our country.

As nearly as I can judge, although these men are practically all college men and well educated, they do not represent, excepting in a very few cases, the moneyed class or millionaire element in the states. They are representatives of the well-off middle class. It would seem that the very wealthy prefer to save their necks & money and to allow the other fellow to shed his blood. I cannot say about the working class in the states, but judging from what

I have observed so far the men who have volunteered their services in behalf of this country are those who spring from the middle class at home.

October 10, Tours

A beautiful morning, brisk and snappy, with a very slight wind from the SW. At sunrise every plane was out scurrying across the field and sailing through the air. My trip this morning was particularly pleasant and encouraging. I am now able to feel the motions of the planes and the necessary maneuvers of the martial bullet are becoming more natural and mechanical. It is, without a doubt, the best sport yet.

The all-important question about camp is when are we to be paid? All of us are broke and payday has long since passed. The meals are terribly monotonous. Never have I been forced to eat a poorer variety. We get some kind of boiled gristly meat with white beans for lunch, and the same meat with mealy potatoes for dinner. The French are supplying this truck, and they certainly are slipping it over the SOS. I have eaten French food for seven months, but never anything like this. However when we are paid, if we ever are, I am certainly going to steer clear of their grub.

October 11, Tours

"Don't pull on zee steek! You fly to keel. Three women love me nobody loves you." We all have French instructors, and it is mighty funny the way they bawl you out. To teach a new man is far from child's play & highly fraught with danger. Benausch is the most famous moniteur of them all. He will get into his plane with a new man & tell him to own it. The results often take your breath away. He has another habit of turning around & slapping a man in the face who is not flying correctly while sailing through the air. The tales of his actions are many, and he is undoubtedly a very nervy proposition.

October 12, Tours

The days are now becoming a great deal colder and the weather more unsettled. It is a very easy matter for us to see our breath in our quarters and the mess hall. When off duty or when the weather does not permit us to fly we spend our time reading in bed well covered with blankets, and we have already begun to curse the cold. A very foggy cold is the most penetrating proposition I have ever experienced, & this county seems to be the most humid in the world. I can only speculate as to what our experiences are to be when winter really sets in, and I am quite sure that we will not forget the winter of 1917-1918. However, I am looking forward to it as decidedly different if not pleasant, but I do not want to see a reproduction & the severity of last winter.

October 14, Tours

Rumors are always prevalent in an organization of this kind. Some are well founded and others are not. The "hot stuff" about camp at present is that we are all to be rushed through our training with the greatest possible celerity and are to be sent to the front by Christmas. All eyes are now being turned to the U.S., and our record is to be watched very closely both by our enemy and allies. This will stimulate everyone to his greatest effort, and

I firmly believe the fellows in this school will make an enviable record.

Our infantry, that is the first contingent that arrrived here some time ago, ought to be ready to enter the trenches within the month. These men are of our original army and are not the type or men who have volunteered since war was declared. I cannot even venture an opinion on the showing they will make, but feel certain that the next contingent will do well. As for the fellows I have seen in the aviation, I am sure they can't be surpassed by recruits of any other nationality and feel certain that the boche will have cause to remember them.

October 16, Tours

I am now progressing in the aviation game to the extent that I feel perfectly confident and am able to do everything satisfactorily except land. This is by far the most difficult phase of flying, and I am greatly surprised to learn how hard it is to bring a machine down properly.

Everything is going on about the camp as usual. The food continues to be rotten, and the paymaster is sixteen days overdue. Everything else, however, is smooth and satisfactory.

October 17, Tours

Terene is the name of my moniteur, and he is one of the wildest Frenchmen I have ever known. We go out to learn to fly and have the time of our lives. He skims down over trees, chases partridges, killing them by hitting the wires of the plane, races trains and dives down at men working in the fields scaring them so that they scatter in all directions.

Sometimes he wears wooden shoes & while you are busily employed in the effort of keeping the machine right side up he suddenly spies some one below & stands up with a shoe in his hand threatening to throw it at him. The great attraction in Terene is that you never know what he is going to do next.

October 18, Tours

It is wonderful how many accidents can occur resulting in the complete smash up of the aeroplane without hurting its occupants. During the last two days eleven planes have been destroyed and not one man hurt. These accidents usually occur while the machine is being landed by a green pilot, and it is a very common sight to see one turn turtle or pancake down in a thousand pieces.

October 19, Tours

We are extremely lucky in the favorable weather we have been having. It is a perfect Indian summer, and altho the morning fogs are rather heavy, they seldom deprive us of more than an hour's flying. The field and air are actively filled with buzzing aeroplanes practically all of every day.

October 20, Tours

Today we held memorial exercises in honor to the death of Captain Guynemer the French ace of aces. The entire school turned out on the main flying field and stood in military formation while two French officers did the honors. All flags are to be at half-mast for days at all aviation schools, and the entire French nation is in mourning.

October 21, Tours

It is most interesting to listen to the comments of many of the ground school men on conditions at the front. None of them have been out there, nor have they a semblance of an idea as to its real character. Yet, they speak authoritatively of methods used in bombing etc., their statements being so far off as to be ridiculous. You cannot, moreover, explain their errors to them on account of their evil manners. But I am looking forward to the day when they will be suddenly disillusioned, and I will certainly enjoy watching them swallow their exploded theories.

October 22, Tours

The money that I wrote for at Paris a week ago arrived today, and I immediately went to town and ate a good, big square meal. To be deprived of a thing is the greatest possible way to increase your appreciation of it, and to state that I enjoyed myself is putting it too lightly.

October 23, Tours

Life down here has become commonplace, and we have all become accustomed to the general schedule. On bad days, excepting for a forty-five minute lecture on engines, etc., we have nothing to do, yet the time passes rapidly, and we are becoming expert in wasting it. Any life of any kind entails a great amount of lying around, and one quickly forgets the habit of work. I have now had eight months of this kind of life, and it is getting to be a great question in my mind as to whether or not I will ever be able to get down to work again.

When I think back on the days I spent drudging for the Butler Paper Co., I can scarcely imagine how I did it. I am thoroughly convinced, moreover, that I would never again be able to submit to the treatment I received in that slave organization and to think of settling down to an everyday monotonous existence doing the same thing day after day appalls me. Then to carry it a little further and imagine a home in a one horse suburb with a wife whom I would have to look at, live with, and report to during all of my life, it seems impossible and terrible.

October 25, Tours

We were paid today! The paymaster arrived today after a delay of twenty-five days and paid us for last month. We were paid on a basis of $33.00, as the red tape of the government has not yet moved far enough to allow the $100. The whole camp is in an uproar, crap games, poker and confusion reigns supreme. Three trucks leave for town tonight, and the last one returns at 5:30 tomorrow morning.

October 26, Tours

I have just finished a most delicious and satisfactory meal, which I naturally did not eat in the mess hall but purchased in a near-by restaurant. This restaurant is far from pretentious. It has a dirt floor, is lighted by a lamp that gives out a dull smoky light, and its only heat is derived from the cook stove but the food that they cook on that stove is just as good as any that can be bought in the best restaurants of the world. We ate rather lightly? And were just able to stagger home without overflowing. The menu was as follows: beer, ham omelet, two mugs of steaming hot chocolate each, the same portions of toast and butter, french fried potatoes in enormous quantities and steak done to a turn. Can you wonder why I now feel somewhat distended in the abdomen and why a great feeling of content and satisfaction has crept over me? I seem to have but one use for money at the present time and that is the food I can provide with it. I don't know whether or not it is a tapeworm, but if so, he is receiving some royal reports.

October 28, Tours

Our moniteur is at present the most unpopular man in our sphere. He has procrastinated throughout the entire week to such an extent that we have had but one ascension. I don't know why this should anger us inasmuch as we are very comfortable and happy here and should not wish to hasten our death, but the other fellows are getting along a bit more rapidly, and we do not like to see this. However, we will soon be out of his class and into solo work where our fortunes will probably change.

October 29, Tours

The boche have been raising particular hell lately. They are driving the Russians back until they now threaten Petrograd. They have launched a tremendous and unexpected attack against the Italians with the result that they have driven them off of the ground that has taken them two years to occupy and now threaten Italy proper. The submarine continues to be actively engaged, and the air raids upon England continue. The counter efforts of the allies are slight in comparison. The English and French have made some slight advances at considerable costs upon the eastern front. In spite of these facts, the papers speak of the broken hun and of peace at their terms. American public opinion is ignorantly self-confident and speaks of the Christmas dinner in Berlin & of the Kaiser as a supplicating prisoner. People should not be fooled or allow their conceit to deter them from looking at the true situation as it stands. They need to cope with it, realizing and understanding the strength of the enemy, in order to meet the situation and to eventually overcome it.

October 31, Tours

The days have passed during the last week with hardly a suffi-cient variance of schedule to deserve comment. We have adjust-ed ourselves to the schedule of affairs and live as casual an exis-tence as though we were commuting between Hinsdale and Chicago, selling loose leaf during the week and participating in the regular Saturday night dissipation. But when I look back upon my two years with the Butler Slave Co. & six months with the loose-leaf devices, I wonder how I ever stood it. A heyday existence and the bright outlook of a struggling commuter with the exciting recreation of cleaning a cellar and spading the gar-den on Sunday together with greeting the same woman each morning and evening who has been bound to me in holy wed-lock--not for yours truly!

The great question is what will I be satisfied with *après la guerre* providing I get through. My present mode of life, the experiences I have had, and the knowledge I have gained from travel and association, will have rendered me unsuitable for the humdrum existence I will be fitted for. Never will I be satisfied to settle down to such a life, and I look upon the future with some uneasiness. Of course, there is the army, but the greatest point is that there are very good chances on my pushing up the daisies before the war is over. Therefore, the reason I do not talk or speculate upon the future is self-evident. The task before me is to live in the present and in the present only.

November 3, Tours

The contented camp at which I arrived about a month ago has gradually changed into one of sedition and dissatisfaction. The principal grievances are the food, the discontinuance of the trucks to town, the roll call, the vagueness of commissions and the question as to our present rank and pay. A large indignation meeting has been held and the government, the army and the county in general were cursed most prolifically. An announcement to the effect that the school has now become an integral part of the American Army was greeted with howls and grunts of disapproval. Lt. Knight, who is in charge of the school, came down to talk to us this evening and pour oil on the troubled waters. He explained the difficulties of the problem of doing everything at once and was talked to in no respectful tone by the fellows, and has been stirred into action. I feel sure that before long things will be going more smoothly.

November 4, Tours

The men who have been trained in the ground school work have some more serious grievances, and when we compare our lot to theirs we can consider ourselves mighty lucky. A great many of them have been over here two months without seeing an aeroplane, and they are building barracks and digging latrines at Issoudun at the present moment. The condition of the Army of the U.S. is now very similar to that of the British and French at the beginning. No one knows what he is doing, what he should do, or why he has been appointed to office. The result is a vast conglomeration of men eager to do something drifting around aimlessly poorly fed and sheltered doing work for which they are unfitted. You can hardly blame the hun for being scornful and confident. We are impeded by a vast amount of red tape and lack of understanding in the higher offices. Three years example of pain and suffering so far has taught them nothing. I wonder if they will also be forced to learn their lesson on the battle field?

November 6, Tours

I have just learned that Jerry Stevens is down at Issoudun and will eventually be sent up here for his training. I am looking forward very much to seeing him and understand that he is the same old Jerry. Jimmie Buncher is also at Issoudun, and it begins to look like all of the regular fellows will soon be with us. We will sure have a good time, while we last anyway, for they have corralled the live ones in this service and no mistake. I think that the calibre of men in the aviation is to be somewhat different from that in our conscripted army.

November 7, Tours

Gus Denison has been appointed a captain in the O.R.C. and I hear that he is training three hundred men of the conscripted army at Rockford, Ill. Fifty of these men are unable to speak a word of English. Are these men to represent our country abroad? If so what kind of a record will they make, and what impression upon our allies? I can only reiterate my former doubts and am following their record with great interest.

November 8, Tours

This diary seems to be developing into more of an expression of opinion on the part of the writer on such subjects that are of pre-eminent interest to him at the moment rather than a description of daily life. But unfortunately the daily life becomes very much the same from day to day and in describing it once you have everything that transpires for a month. There are the meals, at present exceedingly rotten, the flying which is good sport, then the other small incidents of the day such as the bull sessions around the stove, the kicks, and new regulations imposed by green officers, and the conjectures as to when they will wake up and when we will receive our commissions. The greatest of all events, however, is the arrival of the paymaster and the dip into the society of Tours thereafter. At present, we are all awaiting anxiously his arrival, as he is, as usual, long overdue.

November 10, Tours

Our outlook is at present mighty blue. The boche have made an advance 50 miles into Italy taken a great number of prisoners and are still advancing. Russia is so torn with internal strife that no one knows where she stands and little or no material aid can be expected from her. The English and French have sent men to Italy to stem the tide and try to force back Gen. Mackenson's hordes but little confidence can be placed in them to do more than stop the invasion. The general feeling is naturally quite blue and if these German successes continue I see no alternative other than a premature & unsatisfactory peace with continued preparation for a future war even more gigantic and terrible. The entire world is looking upon these battles with not a little trepidation and interest.

November 11, Tours

The latest rumor about camp has it that the huns have withdrawn their best aviators from the fields and that she will hold them in reserve until next spring when the allies and the Americans will start their greatly advertised campaign in the air.

November 12, Tours

England is scared stiff. Her streets are totally dark at night, the people serious and concerned, and she restricts her people to the most niggardly meals in all of her restaurants. The men who have just come from there say that the difference between England & France is astounding. Perhaps she is looking further ahead than the Frenchmen. At any rate, I am sure she will stick to her last man and I only wish I had the same confident feeling about all the rest of our allies.

November 13, Tours

Jerry Stevens arrived today in the crowd of 94 ground school men who have been groveling in the mud at Issoudun. It looked mighty good to see him again. We walked to town in the evening discussing the questions of the moment as tho we were again walking down the streets of Madison engaged in nothing more exciting than attendance at the U. It is a peculiar but saving fact that one can adapt oneself to abnormal conditions with the greatest of ease and in consequence live as casually as though our lives were being spent in the most commonplace manner.

November 14, Tours

One hundred more cadets have arrived direct from the U.S. This aggregates about 400 flyers in all. Since the school capacity is limited to about 280 the balance are forced to remain on the ground guarding barracks etc. with empty guns and doing K.P. duty. They could not be sent to Issoudun owing to the fact that the entire camp is quarantined with the mumps and even we have two barracks confined for twenty-one days. The mechanics brought this disease from America and it has been so far impossible to eradicate it. The men in confinement are becoming exceedingly restless & are importing liquors as a solace. Several of them, moreover, are sneaking out at night to a nearby village where it is possible to buy a decent meal. This is of course a pretty serious action but you can hardly blame them, considering the food that they are forced to eat.

November 16, Tours

The paymaster arrived today and doled 570 francs per man. The result is a distinct rise in the morale of the camp. We all went to town this evening and celebrated the occasion in the proper manner. Everyone in camp was out in a body and a most enjoyable time was had by all.

Arrived back at daybreak and inasmuch as the fog prevented flying we started the after pay day crap game in which I had the good fortune of gathering in 200 francs to the good.

November 17, Tours

The fog lifted this p.m. and I went out to make my first hop. My feelings were distinctly squeamish when I stepped into the plane alone for the first time with a trip before me the outcome of which might prove distinctly exciting. My instructor had never allowed me the complete control of the machine so I was not exactly sure as to how I would get by. However, these apprehensions quickly vanished when I left the ground and I managed to come down without trouble. Then came two *tour de pieces* and I began to enjoy myself immensely.

November 18, Tours

This class of first *tour de piece* work is better than any circus I have ever attended. Men come down at every possible angle, turn over, wing slip, and crash in a heap. One man by the name of Reed goes up and gets lost on almost every flight. Meanwhile our moniteur raves in a combination of French and American curses. Reed capped the whole situation today by landing head on to a stone wall in a nearby village completely demolishing his plane and escaping unhurt himself thru some miracle of fate. The funniest part of the whole game is that our instructors give us the devil for not landing properly when we do not break anything, but if a man turns over smashing the machine into bits he doubles up laughing at him.

November 19, Tours

A major of some sort has now taken charge of this camp and become distinctly unpopular with all of us. He has put up a cordon of guards about the place and rendered it impossible to get out except during certain hours and with permission. This means that if we are to stay out all night, get a good bath, & sleep in a decent bed, we will have to allude the guards both going out and coming back. Inasmuch as Bill Beaument and I expect to do this tomorrow evening, this journal may contain things of a different strain on Wednesday.

November 21, Tours

I left at 5:00 p.m. and sneaked out over the flying field with a bicycle and made town without difficulty. Here after trying on my uniform I met Bill Beaumont who had done the same thing and we proceeded to enjoy ourselves returning in full daybreak and successfully running the guards after much maneuvering in stocking feet.We now have a major in charge of the school who is lower than W.S. and a 14 karat s.o.b. He informed some of the boys that he was going to make things just as disagreeable for all of us as possible & to pass this word on. He is the same man who brought the sixth platoon over in steerage when they were to be provided with good quarters, transported them to Issoudun in box cars, & made them walk 7 miles thru the mud to camp, sending the trucks which had arrived to carry them back empty. He is putting on restriction after restriction & it is now impossible to even buy a meal that you can eat. Naturally the spirit of patriotism among all of the men has changed to sulkiness & the men who were so anxious to fly under the old regime have become indifferent. This is most unfortunate & I sincerely hope that things will soon come to a head with the result that our dear major is deported.

November 23, Tours

The days are now passing very rapidly. Flying alone is great sport and we live from one flight to another. The landing of the plane is the most difficult phase of flying and there is quite a knack to bringing her down at the correct angle considering that this has to be done at a speed of about fifty miles an hour. A three point landing in which the tail and wheels touch at the same time is the one that has to be learned. If you are forced to come down in the country due to a bad motor, a landing upon the wheels on rough ground would be disastrous.

November 24, Tours

Today is my birthday but my financial condition has not made it possible for me to celebrate in the proper manner. It has turned quite cold and the day is overcast. We have all spent most of our time sitting around the stove gassing and trying to keep warm. The worst time of day is the morning. We all lie in bed until the roll call bugle is blown in most unpleasant anticipation of crawling out of a warm bed into cold damp clothes. The weather in France is extremely humid and it requires the greater part of the day with a hot stove to dry out the barracks. It is at this time before one is more than half awake that he wonders why he has chosen this life and why men are such fools as to fight.

November 25, Tours

I have now been put into the Anzani class. We still fly Caudrons but they are fitted with stationary Anzani motors which are considerably heavier and land much faster. The controls, moreover, are not as sensitive as the Gnome and she is more clumsy and harder to handle.

November 26, Tours

The weather cleared up late this afternoon sufficiently to allow us to fly. I spent most of my time waiting for the mechanics to tune up my plane. They finally succeeded in making it run after a fashion and I started out. I had scarcely reached an altitude of 50 meters when my motor began to poop. For a short time, I was afraid I would crash into the hangars but luckily managed to glide over and looking below saw nothing but an orchard and a vineyard both impossible landing places. However, I managed to reach a small plot of ploughed ground by banking to the right and brought her down without mishap. Two mechanics arrived & again made the bus run. I thought I would try to run her out and fly back to the field as the sun had already set. To do this it was necessary to hold her on the ground as long as possible so as to be able to gain sufficient speed to fly over a nearby farm house. Therefore, I held her on the ground until she was running between 40 & 50 when suddenly there was a crash & I went flying over onto the ground in the machine which had turned a complete somersault. Luckily my strap had held and I was all o.k. I had hit a small furrow in the field, which had due to the speed of the plane turned me over.

November 28, Tours

I am not in a particularly cheerful mood at the present moment so I will endeavor to take it out on this record. I have now been in the spiral class for a week and although the weather has been perfect, I have not been inside of a machine. It is not due to the weather, moreover, but to the lack of machines and here we are all fighting to get along and the most efficient U.S. Government has no machines to offer us. Two hundred more cadets, all of whom have completed their theoretical training, three hundred more are at Issouden, and our officers haven't enough pep to liven up the construction department. Instead of doing this they spend all of their time seeing that our bunks are without wrinkles and that our shoes protrude from under our beds at the regulation angle. Bah! American efficiency, American conceit, bluff, and brag is more like it. Which seems more practical to an animal of the most remote intellect, to feed a man well or to get him up in the middle of the night to do calisthenics? *Merd alors.*

November 30, Tours

Major Christie has now superseded the unpopular commander in this school. He has a very good reputation among the fellows at home. We hope he will make good by doing something sane.

December 1, Tours

Inasmuch as I have only twelve hours and need fourteen before I can go on voyage, I went over to the totalising class and flew an Anzani for two hours. It was great sport; I was at liberty to go where I wished so could try anything I wanted to providing that they did not see me. I climbed up to about 700 meters and came down in a tight spiral whirling around until I lost all sense of direction then climbing up again. It was certainly great sport and I swear by all that's holy that when I get up in my altitude test I am going to try everything from loops to tail spins.

December 2, Tours

The Americans are now so numerous in France that there is scarcely a place you can go without seeing the khaki uniform and the impractical broad brimmed hat. Prices too have jumped as they always do upon the arrival of the American who is known throughout the country to be a fool with his money. He deserves this name moreover, and why he does it I am unable to say. For as long as we have money in our pocket, we throw it away and being without it seems to teach us nothing. I have been absolutely flat broke for two months at a stretch and have been forced to smoke French issue tobacco because of the fact. Yet when I again procured money, it was the same old story. We seem to be perfectly contented to live either on the crest of the wave or at the bottom of the sea.

December 3, Tours

A great many conscripted clerks are now arriving who will be placed in the quartermaster and accounting department. They are typical slow-moving. conservative, conscientious individuals who wear glasses and may be seen each morning and evening sitting quietly on the train running to and from the nearby suburbs. They are the type of men who are perfectly contented to draw their $100 per month and work in the garden on Sunday. Now I wonder what effect France with its easy going customs and women is to have on them. I have seen so many studious, moral, and serious young men change completely that I can't help but picture these men when they return to the States, changed completely and I am very much afraid that their former mode of living will not satisfy them as well as it would have if they had not had this little experience.

Then if we think of the men of the more adventurous and dissatisfied type. The type that is so prevalent in this service and consider that this life will render them even more unsettled and adventurous. I cannot help but feel that the effect is to be felt throughout the world. Standards are going to change and our social scheme must again settle into channels which before the war would have seemed scandalous.

December 6, Tours

The YMCA has now established a canteen in the camp where they provide reading and writing rooms and sell coffee, chocolate, tobacco, etc. It is a very good innovation and the American coffee tastes particularly good. They also provide entertainers on occasion and hold church services on Sundays. The last named has not as yet drawn me, but I endorse the other advantages.

December 7, Tours

I did my spiral today and luckily came out with an almost perfect barograph and landed upon the designated spot without trouble. It is great sport and I enjoyed every minute of it. We climb to 700 meters cut our motor & spiral down. The wires whistle and she careens about very much as a sailboat in a heavy wind.

December 8, Tours

The weather has changed abruptly from clear calm perfect days. A strong south west wind accompanied with a driving rain greeted us this morning rendering it possible for all of us to roll over and sleep through the morning. I have now only my triangles and altitudes to do before receiving my brevet. After that *trois jour du Paris, n'est pas?* And I am just about ready to dip into the Parisian life again. Paris is a city that you never tire of returning to in spite of the fact that a protracted stay will make you wish to move on, but three days is an ideal length of time as you can just about cover the ground without repeating in that time.

December 10, Tours

I had quite a surprise today while walking up to the pilotage I noticed a lieutenant talking to Johnson of the Lafayette Escadrille and upon looking more closely I discovered him to be Ted Merideth. I had not seen him since 1910 but he has not changed in the least and while talking to him I felt very much as tho I was again down at Mercersburg on the ground floor of dorm 88. He trained in the States and received his R.M.A. there. He is now in charge of some of the cadets and expects to remain here for some time.

December 11, Tours

Christmas packages and letters are now beginning to come in. I have received countless knitted articles particularly wristlets of which I have enough to equip an army and all knitted with stitches of love. The women in the States are apparently working their heads off and although the resulting material is not always practical, the spirit that has moved them should be greatly admired. If some of our men were imbued with this same patriotism we could be well satisfied with our country and have few tremors as to the results on the field of battle.

December 12, Tours

The boche are now apparently withdrawing the best of their men from the Russian front where they are no longer needed and massing them for an attack against the French. This is undoubtedly to be a gigantic effort on their part to break down that which is left of the French Army. One cannot help but admire their foresight as the condition of the French is far from strong. I will look upon this attempt with no little uneasiness for the U.S. is not yet ready to be of substantial aid. If the French are broken and forced, out the Germans will be well able to dictate their terms. However, this attack will not be launched as a complete surprise as was the case in Italy. I feel certain that friend boche will receive a mighty warm welcome at the hands of the frogs.

December 14, Tours

The weather cleared today and I started my voyage work. I have an Anzani motor which turns up to only 1150 rpm, but in spite of this, she climbs pretty well and answers to her controls readily. They say that the type of propeller on her keeps her from making the customary 1250 revolutions.

I made my *petite voyage* to Vendome an English airdrome some fifty kilometers north of our camp. I flew the entire distance at an altitude of 800 meters and found the way very easily. Forests, rivers, railroads and all other landmarks take on the same shape, direction and contour as given on the map and on a clear day finding your way is simplicity itself.

December 15, Pontlevoy

I started out on my triangle going from Tours to Chateaudun and from Chateaudun to Pontlevoy. The second leg of this trip is the most difficult as there are no special landmarks by which to find you way. Moreover, I was forced to fly rather low on account of the ceiling which had dropped to about 600 meters. I found my direction, however, by means of my compass and finally sighted Blois and the river Loire. Arrived in Pontlevoy about 3:30 p.m. tired, but with a feeling of having enjoyed myself thoroughly. I could have completed my triangle and arrived at Tours by dusk but I felt that I would prefer to stay in the village that evening so I told the NCO in charge of this post that I was going in to obtain a bite to eat, and I contrived to forget to return.

There are nine of us in this village awaiting favorable weather that will permit our flying back to camp. We are quartered in a small épicerie run by a Frenchman by the name of Benoist. He was chef of the Savoy Hotel in London before the war and sure can cook. We are living like kings and have nothing in the world to do but eat and sleep in big feather beds.

December 17, Pontlevoy

A travelling cinema made a one night stand in the metropolis and we together with the entire population attended a movie that broke and sputtered its way through two reels of pictures that had been made some time back in the dark ages. It was great sport, however, and we would have remained through the entire performance if there had been a bit of ventilation in the theatre. As it was, the fumes of garlic, which apparently the whole town had been eating, conquered us during the last reel, and we were forced to break for fresh air.

December 18, Pontlevoy

The family with which we lived is, I think, typically Provincial French and are as nice people as you can find. Father, Mother, Daughter, Aunt, and the rest all live together in their little old fashioned house. Their tastes are the simplest but their food is plentiful, and delicious.

A Frenchman will deprive himself of anything but his meals from which he derives his greatest pleasure. These people are extremely polite and sociable and have the greatest confidence and good opinion of the American students at Tours. The fellows do not take advantage of them in any way and all who have frequented this place have been the right kind.It cleared up today and we all flew back to school to find that the paymaster had not yet arrived, *Merd*!

December 20, Tours

I have again neglected this text and must tell something of what has happened during the week. A large number of Aero Squadron men arrived. They are mechanics and workers and are to relieve the Frenchmen doing this work in the school. There were no available quarters for them, moreover so we were all forced to get out of our barracks and move up the road to those which are partially completed and are to house the cadets. These barracks, when completed, will be very comfortable and satisfactory. However, at present, they are without lights, & water. Glass has not as yet been placed in the windows and aeroplane linen is tucked over them.

The north wind is blowing a gale & one small stove tries to burn usually without success, but when it does overdo itself, you can see your breath within three inches of its exterior. The weather has turned bitingly cold and we all sit around cursing everybody in the world and wondering why we had not decided to win the victory on the farm. The aviator's dream has suddenly shifted to the blackest nightmare. Water to wash in is unavailable and after several attempts to brush my teeth with snow I decided to become Godly instead of cleanly.

However, a ray of sunshine enters into the abyss in the form of an official notice stating that until further notice there would be no reveille or drill formations and that we are free to go to Tours on the afternoons of the 23rd, 24th and all of the 25th. The paymaster, moreover, is to arrive tomorrow and to pass out the much needed money.

December 23, Tours

After canvassing the camp, a crowd of us succeeded in borrowing enough money to see us through the evening and we bid goodbye to the place with a great good will.

Our celebration of the holidays commences and we all procure rooms in a hotel, said rooms being heated and provided with feather beds into which you sink about two feet. The evening was spent in the cafés and the Alhambra, the music hall of Tours. Then upon waking at nine o'clock in the morning we gently push the bell and have omelet & chocolate brought to our rooms. From famine to feast is a big jump and one which increases the units of satisfaction in said feast one hundred fold.

December 25, Tours

Raise the flag! The paymaster doled out the scheckles today and we all made faces at our new barracks and returned to town with alacrity. This evening was spent very much as the other on the crest of the wave. We also made arrangements for a big Christmas dinner in a private dining room and sixteen of us sat around the festive board of such articles as partridge and champagne. The dinner radiated nothing but good cheer and we all had a Christmas dinner that could only be surpassed by the one at home. Afterward the battle of Tours was raged with quiet ferocity and although there were some casualties the day was won and pronounced a grand success by everyone.

December 26, Tours

Today was rather blue owing to our returning to cold barracks and a desolate camp after having so thoroughly enjoyed ourselves over Xmas. A crowd of us walked out through a driving snow storm to the little village of Notre Dame some 21 kilometers away where we ate dinner and hugged the stove. The party was particularly noticeable for its lack of pep and we finally walked home finding a bright moon above us and the clouds blown completely away.

December 27, Tours

The fellows are gradually straggling in and the camp is again taking on a military appearance. The weather, however, is so bad that no flying is possible. As a result the fellows have very little of interest to occupy their minds and a rather shiftless demoralized atmosphere prevails. However when the gale stops blowing things will again come back to normal and we will once more see an interested gang about us.

Enders, one of the fellows now in voyage work had a very narrow escape while flying over Chateaudun. He turned in a very steep bank and the end of his top wing collapsed. He immediately went into a *verrie* & pulled sharply on the Marshall bullet in an attempt to right his plane. He could not, however, budge the stick, so tried his motor. This resulted in throwing himself upside down. So, preferring a verrie to this position, he coupied & dived head on into the ground. He fell in all 800 meters & only bruised & cut himself quite badly. A pretty lucky boy, I would say.

December 29, Pontlevoy-Chateauden

It cleared today and I started out on my second triangle. A biting cold NE wind blew, however, and a thin haze lay over the ground. I made Pontlevoy in mighty good time, but hugged the stove in the aerodrome for some time before again starting. I then left for Chateauden at about 3 p.m., fighting directly against the wind the whole way. When but half way the sun set and darkness began to set in. A heavy fog rolled over and soon made the ground almost invisible so I peaked slightly with my motor full on so as to obtain a maximum speed and still be able to see the landmarks below me. Then it became so thick that I lost my way even after having descended from 1400 to 600 meters. I was so intent on the ground below while striving to find myself that I came to with a start when I tried to pick out a field below me and could not see what it contained. I immediately cut my motor and came down in a steep glide, luckily landing in a ploughed field below without mishap. I found a farm house nearby where a farmer loaned me his bicycle & informed me that I was but six kilometers from Chateaudun, my destination. I rode into the hotel where I was put up for the night very comfortably. I returned in the morning and flew the plane to the aerodrome, but the weather did not permit my returning to Tours.

December 31, Chateauden-Tours

I left Chateauden this a.m. and tore back to Tours before a ripping gale. In fact the wind was so strong that I was forced to land with my motor full on.

I spent the evening very quietly in the barracks and thought about last New Years Eve, not without a bit of regret that I was not back there.

> This ends my 1917 account lets see how she goes
> through 1918 & how long she lasts— —

French-English Glossary

French	English
abri	dugout, bomb-proof shelter
après	after, behind
arrivé	incoming shell
assis	slightly wounded man, able to sit up
atterrissage	landing
avion de	airplane designed & equipped for
chasse	pursuit and fighting
bombardement	dropping bombs
reconnaissance	taking photographs and reconnoitering
beaucoup	many, much, a great many, a great deal
blessé	a wounded man
boche	popular name for a German
bon	good, fine, all right
brancardier	a stretcher or litter bearer
brevet	officer's commission
cafard	cockroach, slang for "blues"
camion	motor truck or lorry
cantonnement	billet, quarters, cantonment
cave	cellar, hollow
cave voûté	vaulted cellar
cent	one hundred
c'est la guerre	it is the war
chasseur	light infantry soldier
chercher	to look for, to seek
cheval de blanc	ground loop
chez nous	at home
coiffeur	barber, hairdresser
conducteur	driver, ambulance driver

couchés	stretcher cases, severely wounded
coupied	cut engine
Croix de Guerre	French War Cross awarded for bravery
décrochage	stall
défendu	forbidden
éclat	burst, crash, glare, renown, rumor
école de tir	gunnery school
embusqué	a slacker
en repos	in rest billets, behind the lines
épicerie	grocery
espére	hope, expect
glissade	sideslip
infirmerie	infirmary, sick ward
jus	slang for coffee
kultur	German cruelty
ligne de volée	line of flight
mauvais temps	bad, unpleasant, nasty weather
médecin-chef	military doctor or surgeon in charge of hospital or field hospital
moniteur	instructor, monitor
mort	dead
n'est pas?	is it not?
obus	shell
permission	leave or furlough
permissionnaire	a soldier on furlough
petite beurre	butter biscuits or cookies
pinard	wine
poilu	a French soldier
postes de secours	first-aid stations
renversements	turning upside down, reversing
rien a faire	nothing to do
singe	soldier's slang for canned beef

sou	smallest French copper coin, penny
sous-chef	assistant section leader
sorte de vrille	spin
systeme	army organization
taube	dove, German airplane
tirailleur	sharpshooter, skirmisher
torpi	bullet or shell
tour de piece	trip around field
tout de suite	immediately
tout ensemble	altogether
trois jours	three days
verrie	nose dive or tail spin
virage	turn
virage décroché	stall turn
virage glissé	slipping turn
vol en piqué/plongé	nose dive
vrille	spin

1918
War Diary

WWI Events First Half of 1918

1918

Jan.   Wilson presents 14 Point Peace Plan to joint session of US Congress.

Feb.. Wilson makes Four Principles speech to Congress.

March Russia quits war, making peace with Central Power through Treaty of Brest-Livtovsk. Germans launch Spring Offensive: first battle against British at Picardy. Germans advance 40 miles towards Paris and shell city with "Big Bertha". Foch appointed to coordinate Allied actions.

April Royal Air Force created. Germans launch unsuccessful Lys Offensive in Flanders.

May   US Army First Division takes and holds village of Catigny in first American land engagement of the war.. Germans attack across Aisne, capture Soissons, and reach the Marne.

June In first substantial American action, US Second and Third Divisions counterattack at Chateau-Thierry and Belleau Wood driving Germans back across the Aisne. On Southern Front in Italy, final Austrian offensive is stopped at Piave River.

Harvey Conover

First Lieutenant A.S.S.C.   USR

U.S. Air Service

A.E.F.

France

In the event of the above party being bumped off kindly forward this book to—

Mr. & Mrs. L.P. Conover

51 So. Oak Street

Hinsdale, Ills.

Jan. 1-Feb 1, Tours

Owing to my having neglected this record for a month, I will only be able to give a general account of the principal features as they enter my head.

I have now completed all of my brevet tests but one. This is known as a *petite voyage* and is a very short cross-country trip that requires about an hour and a half of actual flying. The weather, however, has turned extremely cold and a blinding blizzard renders flying impossible. We all sit around the stove striving in vain to keep warm or moodily watch the snow sift through the roof down upon our clothes and beds. The "powers that be" have told us in answer to our plea for a roof without holes that they have spoken to Headquarters in Paris of this condition but are unable to remedy it without their consent. We are too disgusted to even curse and our esprit de corps is a negative quantity. "Patriotism" some one remarks sarcastically and he is greeted by a series of growls.

The chief cause of our low spirits, however, is not these physical discomforts, but the fact that Stewart, a young fellow who has been with us during the last two months has come down with spinal meningitis and is now both blind and paralyzed. Noles, another fellow in the barracks came down with the same disease and we are all quarantined until swabs can be taken of our throats for the presence of the germs.

They bring us our regular portion of boiled beef and beans, which we just as regularly throw out without touching, but a man can't stay disgusted forever no matter what the conditions, and we are gradually coming back to normal. We sent out for ham and eggs this afternoon and are now occupied in frying them over the stove. Two bottles of beer apiece have also been smuggled in contrary to the edicts of Uncle Sam and the U.S. Army, and we have enjoyed that food more than anything we have eaten during the last three years.

We varied our program. today by a big game of indoor baseball in which the umpire almost lost his life.

Stewart has died, but Noles is better. Several other cases have broken out and the entire camp is quarantined. The doctor, who is scared to death, tell us that 70% of the cases die, 20% are left in such a condition that they would be better off dead, and the remaining 10% are out of luck. He is a nice, pleasant, sort of an individual to say the least.

We hear the verdict of the swab tomorrow so inasmuch as this is our last evening "toute ensemble" we have rigged up a bar, imported drinks of every variety, so as to satisfy the palates of the most fastidious, and have determined to finish this quarantine in the proper and befitting manner.

The farewell party was pronounced by all concerned as most successful and we find that fourteen or about one third of the crew are suspect and must be isolated three weeks longer. Johnny and I were lucky enough to get out, but Jerry Stevens and several of the rest have to remain.

The fact that the entire camp is in quarantine keeps us from finishing our voyage work, however, altitudes are still permitted, and I have finished this test successfully. I climbed at first to a height of 2500 meters, but a large cloudbank rolled over and I was forced to climb to 3000 meters in order to avoid it. I could then get only occasional glimpses of the ground thru small rifts in the clouds which looked exactly like a solid mass of frozen ice and snow. I lost my way temporarily but after spiraling thru I soon saw the river Loire and the city of Tours to the south of me. When at an altitude of 2000 m. above the camp, I cut my motor and did two *renversements*, the second almost carried me over into a loop and the entire plane quivered & hung in a vertical position momentarily after I again cut. She then swung off into a wing slip & nosedive and I breathed more freely. I again attempted to throw on my motor in order to avoid descending too rapidly, but without avail, and I was forced to come down the entire distance and land in the field with a dead stick.

This sudden change in altitude is said to render landing very difficult owing to the fact that your eye cannot readily become accustomed to the sense of distance. Luckily I was not bothered by this but I experienced a thick stuffy feeling in my head that lasted for several hours.

January, Tours

Life is now nothing but one day after another filled with irritable queries as to when the quarantine will be lifted and when we can get out. Steff Brown has arrived and when he is not flying, he drives the Major's Fiat. He takes him to town every night and then comes back and picks us up. We climb in when the guard is not looking and tear off on a joy ride to one of the towns in the vicinity. Last night we came back full speed as we had remained at Chateau Renault too long when we suddenly upon coming around a turn crashed head on into the iron gate at the Monnaie railroad crossing. The gate smashed open swinging our car, which miraculously remained right side up, directly across the road and bending the fenders almost double. The incident demanded quick action, and believe me, we filled the bill. We pushed that car out, bent the fenders back so the front wheels would turn and shot down the road before the bewildered gate-keeper knew what had happened. The next morning Brownie complained in loud, indignant tones to the head of the trans-portation that someone had bumped into his car after it had been placed the garage. The captain expressed his regret, but told him that such things were often happening and not to worry.

January, Vendome

The quarantine has finally been lifted and I started out on my last petite voyage for Vendome. Upon my way down, I experi-enced no difficulty as I had a strong wind behind me that took me over the distance in twenty-five minutes. While at Vendome, which is an English flying school, I saw a double control machine crash to the ground in a *verrie*, killing both of its occu-pants. Upon my return the wind increased and the rain clouds began to work. The drops of rain thrown back by my propeller cut my face like a knife, and I was forced to drive crouched over in an attempt to fend off some of the rain. The wind was so strong at a thousand meters that I was unable to make any progress in spite the fact that my motor was turning 1250 rpm. I was forced, therefore, to descend to 200 and make my way from that height. When I finally landed in Tours, I was, to say the least, glad to be there.

January, Tours

I spent the next few days lying low about camp in the attempt to wait until Johnny finished so that we could go to Paris together. However, luck finally went against me, and at eleven o'clock on the morning of the 26th I was informed that I would have to leave at noon. The usual chaotic packing took place and three of us took the truck for Tours. Here we ate luncheon and at 3 o'clock jumped on the train á Paris. Our party now numbers four as Hollingers' girl has decided to go with him to the gay city. She is an attractive little French girl whom he met a couple of months ago. She is a milliner and has become so attached to "Hollie" that she spends most of her time nestling up against him in a most unladylike, but characteristically French, manner. She has taken complete charge of him, and I feel sure that we will see very little of him during our coming sojourn. This leaves "General" Strauch and me to pillage the city alone.

January 26, Paris

Our tickets read to Issoudun via Vierzon as Paris is now out of bounds for Americans on leave. This renders our entry rather delicate, and it was quite exciting work dodging the guard upon our entrance. However, I who was entrusted with our ticket, fumbled around until he turned his head, and in about thirty seconds the four of us were speeding towards the Hotel Étas-Unis in a taxi.

After showing, the rest to the Olympic, I started to the opera alone. I met Alice. She is, without a doubt, one of the prettiest girls I have ever seen, and fortunately or unfortunately, one of the most sensible. After the show, I finally succeeded in getting her home, but not without running two taxis out of gas. Crawled in at about 2 a.m. after having the usual bull session at the États Unis with the proprietors and the allied soldiers staying there.

Arose bright and early, that is at 8 a.m. The "General" and I went over to the University Club, which proved to be somewhat of a disappointment. We then drove to the Ritz where I tried to look up my friend Mr. Carter. I found, however, that he and his wife had left the day before for Nice. We then repaired to the Knickerbocker bar to see my friend Louis, who is just the same as ever in his role of barkeep for the Anglo Saxon, who has the plebian habit of drinking over a bar, and who is not noted for his moderate habits. The usual painted ladies were in and out, and Paris is just the same as it was a year ago. We hopped another taxi, rode down the Champs Elysees and out the Bois de Bologne, then back to Invalides, where we saw Guynemer's "Vieux Charles" the little Spad in which he brought down his first 19 boches.

While sitting in the Café de la Paix in Paris drinking the customary aperitif, who should run up but Bill Richards ex section 17, and Joe Keyes ex 16. Bill is the only man in our section who enlisted when the U.S. took it over, and he has just finished a course of training at Meaux, where he was searching a commission. Naturally, old times were passed back & forth, and we almost fell on each other's necks. I learned that Harry Overstreet and Kearfoot had enlisted as privates in the artillery. Norway Hiis is occupied working on the Red Cross garage as a penalty for taking ambulance service leave without turning in his resignation to join the Royal Flying Corps. Red the Killer-Woodhouse is now in England with the R.F.C. Old section 17 was made up of red blooded men and that is certain. The section, moreover, has been cited for work that we did in the two offensives of last summer, and the present members, who have enlisted since, are sticking out their chests & telling of how brave they are.

After lunch of lobster, etc. at Pruniers, I met Mr. and Mrs. Haig & accepted an invitation to lunch with them tomorrow.

The first part of the evening was spent at the Casino with Gaby Deslys & her review of English girls, not to forget the Jazz Band imported from New York, which makes you shed tears of homesickness. After the show, we went to a select dancing apartment that runs on the q.t. and is mighty pleasant. It is located out in Passy & takes an entire floor of a most luxuriously appointed apartment. The only drawback of the entire place is that the champagne, which is its only source of revenue, costs 50 francs a bottle. Here I met a number of Lafayette Escadrille men together with a goodly number of English & Canadian officers, all of whom were mighty fine fellows. Here, moreover, I met my waterloo and thereby lies a tale.

I had not been in the place more than 15 minutes when two touring cars drove up to the door disgorging a crowd of English girls accompanied by English officers. They all came in a crowd following the good old Anglo Saxon custom, and proceeded to take possession. One of the girls played the piano like a streak and we all clustered around the piano singing at the top of our voices. The dance continued until about 4 a.m. and in the meantime, I became acquainted with one of the girls. She plays one of the minor parts at the Casino and is sure a good looker. Also, unlike the showgirl at home, she carries a head upon her shoulders. It may be that I have become very impressionable because I have not been able to associate with a girl of the English speaking race for about a year, or it may be that she is an exceptional girl. The fellows to whom I introduced her seem to bear out the latter statement in their remarks, but as usual I am skeptical not by nature accepting everything at face value.

Be that as it may, the attraction was sufficient to make me spend the rest of my time with the above-mentioned girl taking her to luncheon and dinner, meeting her after the performance, and only leaving her in the small hours of the morning to repair to the hotel for some much-needed sleep. This resulted in my breaking my engagements with my French friend and made me feel as though I was not playing square with her. However, time is so short these days that a fellow is almost justified in spending it as he sees fit and in enjoying himself to the utmost.

Our three days passed so quickly that the next thing we knew we were boarding the train at the Gare D'Orsay and starting on our way to Issoudun. Our spirits were naturally most depressed, and as the French say, we all had *beaucoup de cafard*. At such a time one has a great number of half-settled convictions due to the multitudes of impressions he has had. He lives the past during the next few days until he again becomes settled to the regular routine. I find that each time I return from leave I arrive with different ideas of the country and the people I have been thrown in contact with. I remember well how favorably I was impressed with the French upon my arrival last year. How imbued I was with the spirit of sacrifice, which seemed to emanate from them. They were courteous, sociable, and seemed to carry themselves with a mastered good humor in spite of the blood that they had shed. I confess, however, that this opinion has gradually changed; the courteousness I find is in many cases superficial.

January 30, Paris

The sociability, if not engendered by mere curiosity is caused by their desire to profit from the rich American, and I now view the Frenchman in a different light. He is beginning to remind me of the petty woman who says pretty things to your face but sneers at you behind your back. This observation, I find, is not original with me, but is upheld by others who have lived in this country a number of years. My opinion of the British, that is the Englishman, Australian, and New Zealander (I always consider a Canadian as one of us), has undergone the reverse effect. He says very little, in fact he almost holds himself back from overtures of any sort, but when you do get beneath the surface you find a friend whom you can trust. A man worth knowing, in most cases, is not the one with whom you can become easily acquainted. The Englishman says nothing and plugs, while the Frenchman says a great deal and tends acts in spurts. After all, I think it only reverts to a matter of national customs and habits.

January 31, Issoudun

At 2 p.m. we arrived at a small station and were met by Glen Richardson, whom I last saw at the University about two years ago. He is one of the cadets who is waiting to fly, but owing to the lack of machines he has to await his turn and in the meantime do military police duty. He examined our papers and gave us the latest gossip from camp. We then repaired to the village, which is a typical little French community made up of innumerable tiny shops and cafés, all made of the customary gray stone which defies any attempt at a guess of the time of construction. The usual square with its statue in the center and open urinal at the side, and one or two half-nourished trees, complete the city of Issoudun.

February 1, Issoudun

After having a bath and shave, we went to a little restaurant on a side street run by a motherly and surprisingly active French woman, where we ate a chicken dinner. It banished all fears of starvation and filled us all with a feeling of contentment and satisfaction. A truck took us and our luggage out to the camp., a distance of about twelve kilometers, and after going through the customary red tape of the Army, we went to our barracks where we met a crowd of the fellows whom we had known while at Tours. It certainly did look good to see them again, particularly those whom we had known so well but had not seen for a couple of months owing to our having been quarantined immediately after their departure.

The spirits in camp are exceedingly low, two of the fellows were killed in a collision today. This brings up the total to five in three weeks and there is a mighty big epidemic of nerves among the flyers. To see men killed is one thing, and to see your friends, fellows with whom you have been eating, singing and living, is another. Such cases as these bring a man up with a jerk to the bitter realities of war.

Flying was suspended two hours today in order that the men killed yesterday could be buried. The band marched down the road followed by a Ford hearse and a company of soldiers. Squadrons of aeroplanes flew over the freshly made graves while a funeral march was played and two more of our men were put away.

The camp at Issoudun is unlike that of Tours in every way. The entire spirit is most martial & the strictest discipline is enforced. An American built railroad runs into camp, roads and hangars are being rapidly built & constructed while everywhere there is a bustle that reminds you of a factory town in the states. At the present time this is the second largest aviation camp in the world and in a few months it will be the largest.

Our days are completely filled from morning until night. This is the first time within a year that I have been kept busy for any length of time. Strangely, however, this change is most welcome and agreeable although I do not know how long I will like it. At the present time, the feeling at night that I have put in something beside the day is mighty satisfactory.

We stand reveille at daylight, rush over to the mess hall for breakfast; return to the barracks where we fold our blankets and tidy our bunks. Then the formation for trap shooting, pistol, or machine gun, whichever it may be. At 10:00 one half-hour of calisthenics then lunch, and fly all afternoon. I can imagine no better schedule nor one that I could enjoy more thoroughly. I have always been very fond of shooting and flying is as good a sport as I have ever participated in.

February, Issoudun

Sunday is the only day in the week that differs from any of the others. There is no flying nor are there any formations except, of course, reveille. This does not mean, however, that we are given a rest. Far be it from the Army to commit any such breach. Sunday is reserved for us to stand inspections of every sort in front of a number of officers who attempt to instill us with the fear of God by glaring at us and trying to pick apart our appearance and to criticize the condition of our bunks. Unfortunately, they succeed in terrorizing very few of us, and we remain as complacent and self satisfied as we believe all aviators should. The U.S., along with many other mistakes, tries to treat her aviators as infantrymen and her success is not noticeable. America in this, as well as in everything else, refuses to profit by the example of others, but must learn her own sweet lesson by the clearest of teachers--experience.

After having finished a good meal and a mighty busy day, I must take a few minutes to make a record of passing events as I feel about them in my present mood. The days are passing so swiftly that I lose all track of them until suddenly it is Sunday, we stand inspection, and walk aimlessly about the camp, our time hanging heavily on our hands because we have nothing to do.

We now fly half of each day employing the other half shooting over the trap, on the pistol range, attending lectures on the "theory of flight," and machine gunnery. I am about to enter the single control Nieuport class, having gone thru the grass cutters and double controls. My shooting has improved from day to day and although I am far from satisfied with my present record, I have successfully headed the list in numbers of birds broken.

The weather has been remarkable. Beautiful, warm clear days that remind you of southern California and cold crisp nights that make sleeping a pleasure. The contrast between last year when we had rain, snow, and hail until the middle of April could not be greater and comes as a delightful surprise. This is particularly emphasized to us as Issoudun mud has become historical and morbid warnings have been given that this camp is a trackless swamp during three months of each spring.

I don't know how the famous commission atrocity has escaped this record for it has been the chief subject of discussion with all of us during the last three months. It has been one of the greatest causes of cadet dissatisfaction and low morale among the unfortunate incidents that occurred while we were at Tours, some of which I have given account. Briefly, the facts are as follows. We enlisted in Paris under the understanding that we would, upon the completion of our brevet tests, be made lieutenants. We were, moreover, recommended in these enlistment papers for first lieutenantcies. When we who enlisted in Paris had been at the school of Tours for about at week one hundred cadets from the States arrived. They were picked as honor men, men who had passed their ground school course with the highest grades and were sent to France for immediate training for their efforts. They were to be the pioneers in the U.S. Aviation, they were to be used to train the men who were then enlisting in the U.S. The story of the delays in flying that followed due to American mismanagement has been recorded in my diary kept during the time of instruction.

Approximately a month after our arrival at Tours rumors were circulated about the camp to the effect that we were not to receive the rank that we were promised, but were all to be made 2nd lieuts. The dissention that followed, which was greatly increased by this condition at hand, can only be imagined. I, however, with a somewhat childlike faith in our government maintained that she would not break faith with us and that she would not break the most sacred right of our country that of the right of contract. I, therefore, took but a passive part in the demonstrations against this coming injustice although I gave financial support to the wires sent back to the States in attempts for rectification. A few nights ago, however, I was brought face to face with the cold concrete facts in an interview with one of our officers who is supervising the giving of commissions. I earned this rank when I completed my brevet tests on January 22nd, so when I was called up to his office I naturally expected to receive it. Instead I was asked what qualifications I thought I had which would entitle me to a commission and was told that service with the French Army for six months was not considered equivalent to six weeks training camp at home. I flew up in the air and told said representative in no light terms just what I thought of the U.S. Army as an organization. We had it back and forth for a time until I finally told him that I would be made a first lieutenant or demand my discharge. This came to him as somewhat of a surprise and he pictured my returning home to the folks in disgrace most realistically, but he gasped in amazement when I informed them that I would not return home, but would join either the Royal Flying Corps or the Brazilian Air Service.

This is the way the matter stands at the present time, and it is up to the Army as to whether I remain with them as a First Lieutenant or leave them for the service of one of the allies. I have never believed in being completely subjected to submission by anyone and, although I will put up with a great deal, there are limits to everything. It is now a showdown with our U.S. Army to make the next move.

February, Issoudun

I took my first solo in Nieuport this afternoon and was somewhat keyed up for an exciting ride. I had heard so much about their delicacy of control and the inadvertent *cheval de bois* and the speed with which they land that I expected a thrill from start to finish. I was disappointed in this, however, and experienced nothing but a most agreeable sensation, which was due to piloting a *chasse* plane. They are the greatest thing I have ever flown in and make the old Caudron seem like a freighter.

A short time ago I was boasting about the pleasant weather and comparing it to that of San Diego. Well, yesterday the wind hauled around to the North and yours truly awakened at about 3 a.m. frozen stiff. A cutting wind is blowing and winter is again with us. We flew this afternoon muffled up in "Teddy Bears" and came in thoroughly chilled.

We started our first practice of shooting at a moving target with a rifle at fifty yards. I never realized how difficult such a target is and now know how hard it is to hit a running man. To be successful it is necessary to lead your target from one to two feet. Now when you consider that an aeroplane moves at a speed of 150 miles per hour, you can realize how difficult a target it offers. In order to hit the machine you must lead it at least 40 feet when at a distance of only 200 yards.

There are two organizations in this camp which have been placed here for the betterment of the living conditions of the soldier, namely, the Red Cross & the YMCA. Both have huts and profess to be working for the same ends, but the difference is gigantic. The Red Cross in all sincerity does everything they can for the men, always doing a little more rather than a little less than they prescribe. The "Y" seems to follow the opposite policy. My experience has been that they give a little less for the money and the work is done by apparently able-bodied and, well-fed men in contrast to the R.C., which is run by women. A good score, I think, in favor of the women.

The system of training in this school is such that upon their arrival the students are assigned to sections of approximately ten men, these men are kept together as well as possible throughout their course of training. We have progressed thru the revelers or grass cutters, the 23-meter double control and are now in 23 singles. We have each had six *tour de pieces* and up until today have had the reputation of being one of the best sections in school. Today, however, we lost this reputation by an exhibition of very poor flying. The weather was perfectly clear without a breath of wind. This is a very bad condition as a Nieuport, while landing or taking off, unless steered with the greatest quickness, will whirl around & crash in a second's time. The French call this a *cheval de bois*, which means wooden horse, and is most appropriately named from the horses in the merry-go-round. Two of our men executed this maneuver today turning the planes over and smashing them completely. They have been sent back to double control. We all wonder who will be the next. It is an extremely difficult thing to avoid these accidents and we are all most apprehensive as to our flights tomorrow.

X X X

We were booked to fly this morning at 5:30 a.m. Two blasts of the siren informed us that the weather would not permit it and the spatter of a fine rain on the roof of our barracks informed us why. Consequently, we all gathered around the stove where we had the usual air sessions. The principal topic of conversation is the progress of our country in this war, the conceited self-confidence of the newly-arrived officer, and the impression he invariably makes upon our allies the French and English. We all talk fluently upon this subject and can cite numerous occasions when incidents under our observation have proven our statements. It is a peculiar condition. We curse our officials as a crowd of inefficient, supercilious, grafting idiots, yet let an outsider hint at something of this character and we would be on his neck in a second.

X X X

Today for the first time, since I have been flying a Nieuport I felt perfectly at home. I thoroughly enjoyed myself all of the time in the air as I did in the Caudron. I believe I have now mastered the art of landing the Nieuport.. We have been put forward from the 23 meter to the 18 and all of us are anxious to try our luck tomorrow.

It is most difficult for me to think of this life as unordinary and only at rare moments do I realize that I have not lived in this nomadically adventurous manner all of my life. This whole scheme of affairs is only an accepted mechanical manner of living that seems to be most commonplace and natural. In fact, I often feel that the Harv Conover of U.S.A. was a different person living in a different world. Our friends are killed, injured, lose their nerve, or leave us for some other branch such as bombing or contact patrol. We meet men, become well acquainted, then suddenly we lose them and after having cursed the power that separated us we meet others, and so it goes. All is a gamble and we soon become inured to the extraordinary conditions and become fatalists or indifferent.

There are times, however, when I do not take such a philosophical viewpoint. Perhaps when lying half-awake in my bunk at daybreak when the weather is exceptionally disagreeable and cold and my spirit is at its lowest ebb, I may wonder why men are such fools and I curse myself as being one of the biggest. Cold reason is at such times apt to overrule all spirit of adventure, ambition for fame, and patriotism. Thousands of undeniable facts leer at me until I am wide awake: the tremendous casualties among the allied airmen, the paucity of men who have lasted more than a few months at the front, the inevitable sacrifice that is made of the pioneers in a new army. I am brought back to earth by a two-minute reveille alarm which banishes all such gloomy thoughts, and I think no more of the gloom for perhaps a month when I am again brought face to face with the rosy future by the death of a friend or a similar incident.

The peculiar part of it all is that when I fly these planes that are doing so much damage to so many students, I enjoy every minute of it and think of nothing but the pleasurable sensation of flying a high-powered, delicately-built scout aeroplane.

This morning I made my first flights in the 18 meters and enjoyed myself thoroughly. These planes respond to the lightest touch and tear thru the air so fast that you have made your *tour de piece* before you know it. I made 18 trips and in one half day more, with luck, will finish up & get into the 15 meters, which are the smallest planes built and the most difficult to fly.

This afternoon we were brought up with a grim shock. A. H. Wilson was killed while making his second tour in the 18 meters. While banking on a turn he suddenly went into a nosedive and was killed instantly. "A.H." as we called him, was one of the finest fellows I have ever known.

Twenty-two *tour de piece* today in the eighteens and *fini*. Tomorrow at 10 a.m.. I go over to field 5 where we will fly 15 meters. First we will make landings, then spirals, after that aerobatics and cross-country. Sure am anxious to get into them and to see just how these man-killers fly.

X X X

George Phillipetoux is the next man to leave us. He is, or was, one of the best flyers that has gone thru this school. Because of this fact, when Kiekland the former French tester was killed a few days ago, Phil was given his place. He fell in a *verrie* from 2000 meters and was killed instantly. Phil was about 6 ft. 2, could put on amateur vaudeville, and was a prince of a fellow. This makes two of our pals killed in three days. I wonder who will be the third?

I made my first flights in the fifteen today and certainly enjoyed every minute of it. They answer every little movement and tear off the ground as soon as you open the motor, *Beaucoup bonne.* We have moved to field 5, which is the 15-meter field. The atmosphere is decidedly different, no officers bawling you out, no formations, just a big crowd together doing their best to turn out fliers and all congenial and pleasant. There is no crabbing, moreover, and no debauchery, all realize that they are up against a stiff game and a serious one. No one knows when his best friend is to be among the missing and no one laughingly jokes about it. I have greatly surprised myself by not going out of camp since my arrival almost a month ago, nor have I gone to bed later than 9:30 on any night. I guess I must be losing my speed, but when I do master these Nieuports, it will be time enough to relax.

March, Issoudun

It has rained all day and we have had nothing to do but pass the day as best we can. We sit around the stove doing the famous barracks flying, which consists of the recounting of our experiences in the air of narrow escapes, but since we have come out of them with a whole skin appeal greatly to the sense of humor. This kind of day is the hardest to pass and we write, read, play cards, checkers, etc. Anything to pass the time as there are no outside diversions or places to which we can go.

X   X   X

This morning I experienced a most disagreeable sensation, and the first of its kind I can remember. It consisted of a cold chill up and down my back and a peculiar empty feeling in the pit of my stomach. It was caused by the narrowest escape I have had from "old man gravity" since my debut in the flying world. While taking off in landings #2, which is about two hundred yards from landing class #1, I had some slight trouble with my motor and was completely engrossed in the adjustment of the magnetos. When I finished this operation, I had reached an altitude of about 300 feet and looked up to get my direction. The instant I lifted my eyes I saw a plane heading directly at me and already so close that I could see the pilots eyes. He saw me at the same instant, and if his expression told how he felt, I don't envy him. However, there was no time for meditation and I yanked on the stick shooting my plane skyward while at the same instant he nosed for the earth and we missed each other by a matter of inches when a collision would have meant a band, slow music, and two wooden crosses. Strangely, I did not think of the narrowness of the escape until a few minutes transpired then the true impact of it gradually dawned upon me and the aforementioned feeling crept in. It's alright to put on a front and say you care nothing for such a detail as death, but after a glance at him, life seems mighty good. But the old luck held, so we now have another little experience to remember and enjoy.

X X X

The next hump was the spiral, which is done from an altitude of 1000 meters and is quite difficult owing to the position you assume, which is exactly vertical. Your rudder then becomes your elevator and you whirl around in a tight spiral continually playing with your feet to prevent a stall, *verrie*, or nose dive. I luckily finished up on my fifth and was passed.

X X X

Two cross-country trips and an altitude test today left me very tired and ready to sleep. The old saying about pride and fall, however, was well brought out. When at a height of 12,000 feet I *coupied* and came down in spirals right & left, nose dives, and gyrations of every kind. I certainly considered myself good and admitted it to myself on the way down. Then after some very fancy S work I dived down to land, reversed a little too soon, hit a bump on the ground and bent the lower right hand wing. Unfortunately the French instructor had been watching me and accordingly gave me hell for not making a *tour de piece* in order to accustom my eyes to distances for it is impossible to land well when dropping from such a height. He also informed me that aviation was not a sport, but a serious business in which one should do nothing spectacular when not necessary. The cross-country trips were fairly short and I made them both in the afternoon. Next <u>aerobatics</u> then over the big hump.

X X X

I did my aerobatics this afternoon. They consisted of two *verries*, dropping 200 meters on the first and 400 meters on the second. This maneuver is easily executed, but whirls you around so rapidly that you have no idea where you are when you come out. Four *renversments* are the next in order and are great sport the first time you try them. You go shooting over on your back like a flash and fall out going in the opposite direction. Then the *vertical virages* and wing slips, the latter giving a most unpleasant sensation as you drop like lightning and the entire plane quivers under the tremendous strain. Great care, moreover, must be exercised in coming out in order to avoid breaking your wing. On my right hand wing slip I became too ambitious, and as a result went over on my back falling suspended from the straps only. I brought her out after having fallen 800 meters and within 400 of the ground.

Another fellow was killed today. He lost control when in a spiral and crashed. Am glad I did not know him.

I am now at Field 7, known as Valentine, where we fly formation and reconnaissance. Believe me, we fly too. There are seventy

120 h.p. Nieuports and about 20 of us to fly them. The only reason they let us come down at all is because a plane has to be filled with gas and oil every three hours. I had an interesting experience this weekend. While flying in a formation of five that was to last about fifteen minutes as it was then time for lunch, I was the last man on the right, and the man in front of me picked up the wrong leader. The remaining two planes did not show up and the three of us started across country. My machine threw oil in vast quantities, back on my face and goggles, rendering my vision so hopeless that it was all I could do to hold my position.

After about twenty minutes the man in front of me dived down apparently on a forced landing and, after some few minutes, I closed in on the leader and found it to be an 18 meter with two men in her. I immediately looked back for my companion but could not find him. Then a glance at the country below assured me that I was completely lost. I had the alternative of landing to find out my location or to follow the 18. But takeoff after landing entails cranking of the motor and as the compression is very great, it requires two trained men to crank her so landing was out of the question. Nothing to do but follow the ship before me and wish that I had had lunch.

After about forty more minutes of this I began to recognize the country and I opened her wide, landing at Tours about three minutes later. Here I met Bobbie Cone, Doc Holden, and the rest of the crew and was sure glad to see them. After telephoning Issoudun and telling them I would be back the following day, I borrowed money and clothes, and we all went to town. A good time was had by all.

The week has passed with seven perfect days and yours truly flying every minute until the sight of an aeroplane has become obnoxious. Formation flights are particularly tiresome work as they require continued manipulation of the throttles in order to hold a position, but in spite of this, it is good fun. We sail about two thousand meters above the ground so close to each other that you can distinguish the most minute details on the other planes. A man laughs at you, makes faces, or sticks his finger to his nose, and you return the compliment while you watch him go up and down, up and down, and hold your position similar to his. I led a formation of five this a.m. with a triangle of three well above us for protection, as beautiful a sight as you could see. We held this group for one hour and a half as we soared over the country travelling in all about 150 miles.

The movie man also arrived, and we performed for him by flying low above his camera.

General Pershing and Secretary Baker arrived this a.m. on a tour of inspection, and we flew over the field in a formation of twenty. Every available ship in the school was in the air, and they were as thick as a flock of black birds doing every kind of stunt known in aeronautics. Armstrong, one of our fellows while performing on a "gurn" cracked to the ground and is not expected to live. Butler, a fellow from Tours, who was in my class there, crashed in one of his first flights in the eighteen and died in a few hours. I had hoped that this week would be without casualty but was disappointed upon the last day.

After finishing a formation in the morning, I heard my name called and found that I had a chance to fly to Tours again so immediately after luncheon I flew over to main camp where I secured my pass and in twenty-five minutes landed in Tours. The trip runs along the Cher and Loire rivers, which are dotted with chateaux, villages, forests, and cultivated fields, which appear like a great picture below you. Flocks of ducks, geese and storks were very plentiful flying in my path, but as soon as they perceived me, they scattered in all directions as though bewildered at my presence in such an unknown place. While at Tours I enjoyed myself thoroughly with the fellows and was exceedingly loath to return late Sunday afternoon.

This morning five of us started out on a formation flight on which we climbed to 5,200 meters, far above two layers of clouds. The cold was intense, and we all had a feeling of lightness while our planes wobbled about in the thin air answering to controls sluggishly and losing a great deal of speed although our motors were wide open. We became separated coming down as we dived through two layers of clouds, and our ears became so oppressed from the heavier air that we could scarcely hear the sound of our motors.

The nurses at the Chateauroux hospital held a dance for us this evening so we all "policed up" and tripped over the floors of the hospital to the tune of a squadron jazz band. Can't say I had the time of my life. There were at least four men to every nurse and so the affair was of the cut-in variety. The amount of dancing was very limited. There were, moreover, about four of the women who could dance. Then some of the boys in order to appear military wore spurs, which they flourished about with terrible results. It seemed very peculiar to talk to American girls again, and I could hardly become accustomed to it.

We moved to field 8 today, which is the new field for combat work and is to eventually take the place of Cazo. At present, however, there are eight busses for twenty-five of us, and as the policy is to give one machine to each man, we have to sit around and wait until more arrive. Funny how everything runs to extremes.

My commission has finally arrived and it is a first lieutenancy so this score is settled. I went over to summary court officer this evening prepared for battle in case they offered me a second lieut. My last stand must have had some effect for they did not offer it. Now the next thing to see is whether a boche will get me before I get him for I have refused all offers as an instructor or tester. I can't agree with those fellows who figure that they now want to instruct us as the front looks too dangerous.

This seems to be developing into more of a morgue record than a diary for the fellows are now dropping off one and two a week. "Whitie" was killed today at Cazaux while practicing gunnery. His plane collapsed in midair. Whitie hailed from Chicago and was some boy!

Paris has been shelled from the German lines! When I first heard this I refused absolutely to believe it, but it is true, and I guess we will have to take off our hats to the Hun. Although the material damage being done by this gun is slight, the moral effect is tremendous. I sure hope the airmen will soon be able to locate and destroy it. You can shell or bomb London forever without fazing the Englishman, but the Frenchman is of an entirely different make up and when you hurt Paris you hurt him.

The boche offensive has started and they are hurling innumerable men against the English who are slowing retreating against them. I hope that they are retiring advantageously and killing more than they are losing. Rumor has it that two American divisions are with them. *Je espere.*

X X X

Life goes on here very much the same as usual. We have a great gang of fellows and something amusing is always happening. Babe Ewing, Bunny Merz and I took a trip to Orleans over the week end and had the time of our lives. Bunny is one of the funniest fellows I have ever known. He kept us in a state of hysterics all of the time. Orleans is overflowing with refugees from Paris frightened away by the bombardment, which still continues. The boche are still advancing and the situation is very grave.

April 1, Issoudun

Great excitement now prevails. A cordon of guards has been thrown around the camp, and everyone is trying to find the man at whom some sixteen shots were fired by our illustrious guard. He is described as being a tall thin man who has the disconcerting habit when under fire of running and squatting by turns thus eluding all of the well directed bullets. The Captain of this field has by his quantities of bull worked the men into such a state of nervous excitement that they see things to shoot at throughout the night thus rendering our sleep most difficult. I fail to see who would be so foolish as to want to get into this camp, and would be very much surprised if anyone is actually seen or caught.

April 7, Issoudun

This noon, Saturday, Johnny and I left for the town of Issoudun where we took a much-needed bath, then settled down to enjoy ourselves at the Café Americain, thus named in honor of the men of the U.S. who are so free with their money. We had scarcely become acquainted with said emporium when an M.P. came rushing in & said we were to report at camp *toute de suite.* So nothing to do but jump into a fliver and tear out to HQ where we were informed that we were to leave for Cazaux, the gunnery school that evening. Then followed the usual chaotic packing and rushing around to get away.

Finally twenty of us boarded the 10:05 train & started on the journey south. At midnight. we arrived at Limoges, where we changed and jumped on the Bordeaux express, where we found just enough room to stand and looked forward to spending the entire night in this manner. I jumped off at the first station, therefore & ran ahead in search of unfilled compartments. Near the front of the train I found two whole compartments entirely vacant so I yelled to some of the fellows in the rear and Mal Leach, Pop White, Pinkie Ellis, & Pat Patterson ran up and hopped on just as the train pulled out. We then settled down & slept until 7 a.m. Looking out at this time I, of course, recognized the country and informed the fellows that we would soon be in Bordeaux, but eight o'clock came around, then nine, and the country became wilder. The train began to puff up steep grades, and the people appeared to be of much darker complexion. Finally, at a small station I inquired if it was far to Bordeaux and received a reply in the affirmative that nearly knocked me over. "Oui monsieur c'est trois cent kilometers."

When I told the rest of the gang, however, they were far from displeased and thought it a mighty lucky thing. We then had a council of war and decided to remain on the train until we arrived at some good sized city, for if we had to wait for another train it would be exceedingly stupid to spend the time in some tiny village. Meanwhile the country gradually became more mountainous and beautiful. Far away peaks were dotted with ancient strongholds while quaint little villages snuggled in the green valley.

About ten o'clock we arrived at Agen, a city of 30,000 inhabitants, and decided to get off. No sooner had we arrived in the station when a gaping curious crowd gathered around us, and we realized that we had hit a city to which Americans were strangers. We next inquired at to our whereabouts and learned that we were about three and one half hours from Bordeaux, and that the next train left at 4:55 p.m. Therefore, we repaired to a nearby hotel where we washed up and sat down to a long delayed and highly appreciated breakfast. After this, we did the promenade act about the town and again found ourselves the butt of inquires and curiosity. The town is prettier than the average being located in a rather hilly but fertile country. The buildings are artistic and the residences remind one, with their well kept lawns and gardens, of a prosperous American community excepting, of course, that they portrayed the French taste and style, which is so rare in the States.

We had a most enjoyable time answering the inquires of the Agens and were extremely loath to leave when our train came in. The people in this community did not show the effects of the war as vividly as those in the north. Civilian garb was quite noticeable and less mourning apparent.

We arrived at Bordeaux that evening and left the following day for Cazaux.

April 9, Cazaux Ecole de tir aerien

Arcachon, a resort town some seventeen kilometers from Cazaux and situated upon a small lake but a short distance from the sea, looked like heaven to us who had been stuck in the mud hole Issoudun for about two months. Upon our arrival at about 5 p.m. we phoned out to Major Robinson, who is in charge of the school, and acquainted him with our belated arrival. He told us to remain in town over night and to come out on the six-thirty truck the following morning.

The town is made up of a great many villas and summer places, while the shore of the lake is dotted with excellent hotels. A pier runs out some two hundred yards into the water, a promenade lined with benches, and shrubbery is already well used by the populace. A number of sail boats and small craft moored off the main beach make me itch to get into them, and the entire effect is exceedingly picturesque and delightful. One is constantly reminded of the fact that the country is at war even here, however, for the casino once a pleasure resort and rendezvous for gamblers is now a convalescent hospital, and many of the villas are painted with "to rent" & "for sale" signs. It is still, in spite of the wars ravages an attractive place, and I can easily imagine how delightful it was before the war. The continued bombardment of Paris has caused a great many inhabitants of that city to seek shelter in the south, and Arcachon has drawn more than her share of beautiful women who insist upon promenading, thus disturbing our equilibrium and moral balance.

We were rudely awakened at 6:00 a.m. by the bell boy, tumbled into our clothes, and ran for the truck muttering dark and dire curses upon all armies and wars. Within an hour, however, we had eaten breakfast, arrived at the *ecole de tir,* and our interest in things military was reawakened.

In 1915 Cazaux, that is the land upon which the school now stands, was a trackless swamp. Drained by a system of ditches, rendered possible by the sandy soil, it is now considered the best aerial gunnery school in the country. Three thousand men make up the retinue of the camp when running at maximum capacity. Guns ranging from 22 caliber to 3 inch are constantly peppering into the lake and making a din almost equal to that at the front. The flying field, although rather small, is exceedingly smooth and well cared for but it is surrounded by lakes & forests of pine on all sides so that there is no other possible landing place. Therefore, it behooves the pilot to either keep within gliding distance of the field or run the risk of landing in the ocean, lake, or forest, if his motor should poop. The men who fly here, however, are well advanced in the work so that accidents of this character are comparatively rare.

The first two days were spent by us in shooting and lectures. We shoot twenty-two's at paper targets. Then carbines at floating objects in the water and machine guns & carbines from a moving motor boat, the latter being valuable to accustom one to shooting while moving. The slow speed of a motor boat even necessitates a considerable target lead at a distance of 200 meters. The lectures cover the machine gun & deflection.

We have now started upon parachute work to accustom ourselves to maneuvering about an object. We climb to an altitude of 1800 meters and throw out a parachute by going into a virage then circle about it lining up our sights upon it & diving down as it descended. Theoretically this training is very fine, but we are given machines that are in terrible shape, nose heavy, tail heavy, landing wires for flying braces & the wings so weak that one can break them by merely pressing upon their tips. Two fellows in the preceding group were killed by their planes collapsing in mid air so you can believe that we inspected them extremely well before flying & did nothing but straight *ligne de volée* work while in the air. Several of the planes we flatly refused to fly, one in particular with three broken ribs in the lower wing caused so much criticism that the news reached the Major and thereby hangs a tale.

One afternoon after flying we were all called down to HQ and ushered en masse into the Major's presence. He is a West Point man, but unlike most of his colleagues, is a fluent talker. He is, judging from his pronunciation a Southerner, he is well set up and striking looking, if not actually handsome. He is, moreover, very fair, lenient, and exceedingly popular. At this moment, however, he was mighty excited about something and seemed to be scarcely able to keep his chair. We were not long in finding out the cause of it either for he immediately launched forth into a tirade that took us completely off our feet. It seemed that the French had reported that we had purposely broken the wing of a plane because we did not wish to fly it. He, not questioning the report, began to tell us in no light terms exactly his opinion of us. After some difficulty, however, we explained the matter and convinced him that the French had lied concerning the plane and proved to him that the wing had been broken before we had seen it. Things were then smoothed over and we told him of the existing conditions, the final upshot being that several of the old wrecks were taken off the line, and we now go up with a slight amount of confidence in our machines.

Our work on stationary balloons has now commenced. They are allowed to float at an height of about 200 meters and are held in place by ropes from the ground. You fly around in a circle & dive down upon them shooting when you are as close as possible without running into them. It is good fun for in order to make a good score you must get very close. To do this you have to be on the alert every minute and gun over at the last second. If you should run into one of these balloons while at this height, it would mean a spill–a spill with slight chance of recovery before encountering terra firma. To hit it, moreover, while diving it is necessary to aim well below on account of the ensuing deflection.

After the balloon work, we have been put on the sleeve. This is a cloth sleeve-shaped object the size of an ordinary fuselage and is towed by a bi-motor Caudron. Our sleeve has been pulled at an altitude of 2500 meters, and follows a straight line from the lake to the ocean & return. Our Nieuports, which we use in this work, are in good condition and about twice as fast as the Caudron so the shooting is extremely difficult. We *virage* around it, climb on it, dive down on it, shooting when we pass, and watching our tracer bullets for corrections. It is the best practice we have had and should prove to be of invaluable assistance in aerial combat.

I feel pretty conceited and puffed up today for Patterson and I just came within one percent of the school record on the sleeve. We put in 21 balls, which gives us 9.9%. The Frenchmen who shot at the other sleeve put in one ball and feel fine about it. So far at this school, the Americans have beaten the French by a large margin both on the balloons & the sleeve, and I only hope that we will continue the good work at the front.

Today being Sunday, we all went to town, and I think I had as good a time as I have had in a mighty long time. A Franco-American entertainment was held at the casino and I had the pleasure of hearing an honest-to-gawd American band for the first time in some fourteen months. Then I was fortunate enough to learn that my friend the Madame had returned from Biarritz, so we took dinner at the Hotel Regina then movies & I returned on the 10:15 truck.

May 1, Cazaux-Bordeaux

Bunny Merz, Buck Freeman, and I while shooting on the sleeve today broke the school record of 11% by raising it to 13.3%. This brings our average well up and makes us feel very good.

We have now finished our course and are ready for the front with no immediate prospect of getting there owing to the lack of machines. There are now about fifty of us in all awaiting chasse planes. We will be the first to go to the front when they see fit to equip us and a sorry number compared to the 20000 who were to be out fighting at this time.

Off for Issoudun! Them's sad words and no mistake. However, we have all decided to take four days en route and accordingly scattered to all points from Biaritz to Paris. I have decided to remain in Bordeaux then go direct to Issoudun.

While in the QM department getting my pay voucher, I bumped into Homer Etting. Never was I so surprised in my life. About seven years ago he and I went to Mercersburg together, and this is the first time I have seen him since then. He is a private doing some kind of office work, and I don't envy him his job. We took dinner together this evening & had quite a reunion.

I spent the day roaming around the city. It is completely filled with American soldiers and sailors, in fact English is as common a language as French and officers seen everywhere.

I met the girl this evening, she came down from her villa in Arcachon as per agreement and I was naturally very happy to see her. The next two days flew by before I knew it, and Tuesday night I found myself on the train bound for Issoudun in a ugly humor, down on everyone in the Army who invented the place and upon myself for going back.

May 7, Issoudun

Arrived in Issoudun Tuesday morning and upon going out to camp I learned that they had nothing whatever for us to do. We are now ready for the front but there are no planes ready for us, and we must now sit around indefinitely and await development. Here we are the first to finish and it is now May. According to our government's announcements last year we were to have 20,000 planes at the front by Spring. I have never in my life been so disappointed.

I have spent the last three days eating and sleeping and have become more intensely disgusted daily, but this afternoon we were allowed to go over to field 8 and get some more flying as at the present time there are more planes than students. This gives matters a brighter outlook for the planes are good and the practice will be valuable while the time will pass more rapidly.

Two fellows have been killed since I have been here, one I was well acquainted with, Harry Colburn, the other got his over at this field this morning.

Four more were knocked off today. The cemetery popularly known as field 9 is, becoming very popular.

X X X

Bunny Merz, Buck Freeman, and I went out in formation this afternoon, flew over near Tours, circled around the chateaux of Chanson, then went to the flying field at Pontlevoy, where we did every kind of acrobatics conceivable until they stopped all flying and gathered around to watch us. We then flew over to the Chateau Chambord, which is near Blois and the largest edifice of this nature in France, we dived down upon this building while the inmates rushed out to see us. We then returned to Issoudun, after having thoroughly enjoyed ourselves.

This evening fourteen of us received notice that we were to pack up and get ready to leave for the front tomorrow. This is all well and good, but the news that we were to fly observation planes is one of the greatest disappointments I have ever had. They are slow and rickety, you can do no acrobatics or maneuvering with them without losing a wing & they are about to be discontinued for work at the front. After having worked like hell to get into chasse work and after having completed the necessary training, this comes as a terrible blow and all of us are down in the mouth. From chasse to Sopwiths is indeed a fall, and all because they have nothing else for us to fly.

May 11-13, Paris

We left for Paris this p.m. and upon our arrival found the same old city. The statues and historical buildings are protected with sandbags, the windows reinforced to protect them from shells, blue lights have taken the place of the white, but it is all done artistically and the same life goes on undisturbed. We had an excellent dinner at Pruniers, put up at the Grand after having seen the Olympia, and felt much better. We were to leave the following evening, but Johnny missed the train. As his finances were low, I waited over for him while the rest of the gang went down. We followed on the express at noon the next day and had a beautiful ride thru the champagne region over to Gondrecourt. There we called up for transportation and were taken out to Amanty, our destination.

May 14, Front–Amanty

Here we found the crowd and more bad news. Major Dunsmore is in charge—enough said—we fly Sops—nothing but the floor to sleep on, and gawd knows when we will be able to be transferred—oh hell.

We tried the Sopwiths this a.m. and nearly passed out. You can't bank, peak, or virage, without losing a wing so we love them just like a sore thumb.

Bunny, Buck, Johnny, Pat & I walked to Gondrecourt where we found a swimming hole & all dived in garbed in nature's own.

Lufbery was brought down today and Dick Blodgett yesterday. The latter was with me at Tours. I met Luf coming down here on the train to join his escadrille, which is not far from us. He was formerly with Lafayette & had 18 official Huns. A hell of a nice fellow and one of the most popular among all of us.

This record seems to be developing into a record of deaths and a safety valve for my own feelings. I am too thoroughly disgusted to write to people at home, so I must take it out on the birds who

gave us these machines. The French have discontinued the use
of Sops at the front, and as near as I can find out, through dili-
gent research, the only one who likes them is the Hun. They
have killed about as many pilots as he has & our government is
ordering more to bring up the average. As far as being killed is
concerned, I can surely expect that everyone, who stays in the
game without taking a kee wee job, gets his sooner or later, but
all I ask for is a chasse plane, and I will be perfectly satisfied to
play the losing game against fate and old man gravity.

May 22, Amanty

Well, I am gradually becoming accustomed to this place and the
life of ease and indolence. We now spend about all of our time
doing nothing at all for we almost never fly. We get up at 8 a.m.
or later and proceed to kill the day while we all hope that in
some unforeseen manner some chasse planes may turn up so we
can go out and do battle. Kurtze of the 95th was bumped off
today, perhaps there will soon be room for us.

Hathaway, Pike and two others came in today to make up our
quota of 18 men. The observers have not arrived, however, nor
will the planes be equipped with radios for at least a month. I
hope by that time yours truly will be flying an *avion de chasse*.

We are located in a section about 6 kilometers from Amanty and
thirty from Neufchâteau. It is a very hilly country and at this time
of year when all the foliage of the country is in full bloom as the
result of generous rains and sunny days, it is exceedingly beautiful. We are on the border of the Meuse and the Vosges while
directly to the north of us is the Luneville sector now being held

by our first troops who are doing very well considering their experience. Last night we heard a very heavy barrage and upon

Amanty May 1918. Conover (3rd from L) relaxes with friends. Only other identified is Hathaway (5th from L).

climbing the hill, we could see star shells shoot up above the horizon. Today we learned that a small action had taken place in which the Americans showed up to good advantage.

John Mitchell has been bumped off. He was a friend of mine at the U of W & was in the 94th Aero. It is peculiar how we are becoming calloused to the deaths of our friends. Someone comes in and remarks casually that so and so got his today. He receives the reply, "Is that so? Too bad. How'd he get it?" Whereupon details are given, there is a discussion as to his personality and the matter is dropped. All of us, although we hope to get through, now realize how little chance we have. The very best of the airmen are being killed daily. Men whose prowess is far in excess to ours. And we can't help but realize how slight our chances are. Yet, we persist in cursing our luck because we are not engaged in chasse work, the most dangerous of all, and we continue to refuse the offers for bombproof jobs. I don't attribute this to courage but think it is rather the result of a certain undercurrent of fatalism which we possess unknown to ourselves. We all think that we will get it, but all persist in trying to find out when.

June 1, Amanty

The boche have started another offensive and through three successive days have advanced up to Chateau Thiery, which is only 80 kilometers from Paris, the situation is serious. In fact, matters are at a crises and we can only sit around like a crowd of women and hope that they don't get through. This makes us doubly enraged because of the elaborate training we have had but *rien a faire.*

I am neglecting this record terribly but have not been in any mood for writing. We have done practically nothing, are flying poor planes, and I am thoroughly disgusted so cannot bring myself to writing as this is enough of a cursing record when I am in an average state of mind.

Ourches June 13

We remained at Amanty until today when we packed up and flew over to Ourches, our new quarters, some fifteen kilometers from the front where the boche sausages are in sight. We will soon start to work, at least rumor has it so, and believe me, I will be glad to have something to do.

June 16-17, Nancy

Johnny, Lee & I secured weekend passes and spent the time in Nancy. Nancy was a town of 120,000 before the war and was considered one of the nicest cities of France. It is now only a few kilometers behind the lines and, owing to the numerous bombing raids, all but 20,000 people have fled. However, the largest stores and cafés are open and we managed to have a very good time. The destruction done by the Goths is most extensive around the railroad station where whole buildings have been demolished and some are held up by great wooden props. The walls are scarred and torn by *éclat* while the majority of the windows have been smashed. *Abris* built under the streets are numerous, yet the city still retains a great deal of its beauty and attractiveness. In fact, the three of us managed without difficulty to have a mighty good time.

June 18, Ourches

Arrived at Ourches after a nine-kilometer walk and spent the majority of the day sleeping as a continuous rain prevented all flying.

June 19

I took my first trip over the lines today incidentally receiving my first baptism of archies. It sure gave me a thrill as we wandered right over three boche batteries, one of which almost got me. In fact, two or three shells crashed so close to me that I ran through the smoke and looked furtively at either wing fully expecting to see them full of holes. However, I soon dodged out of range & after the reconnaissance returned *à chez nous.*

June 20

Spent the day testing my wireless. As we have a green Radio Officer who, moreover, is afraid to leave the ground, it took much longer than necessary. Finally we found the trouble and put my hack away. It is the first ship in the squadron to be equipped with wireless in working order.

June 21

Arose at 4:00 a.m. and went on "alert" duty, which lasts from dawn until dusk. The plane, the crew, and pilot must be in readiness during this time for an immediate departure, but rain and continued *mauvais temps* prevented any missions.

June 22

Continued bad weather keeps us on the ground again today and I have done nothing other than look over my bus, participate in the usual bull sessions, and take things easy. Baylers is reported missing today. He had some twelve boche to his credit and was with the legion.

June 23

Another bad day with *rien a faire.* In the evening, we went to an entertainment at the Red Cross Hut given by the 26th division representatives. It was mighty good, and I enjoyed it a lot. Major Dunsworth, our CO, is leaving, we also hear the rumor that four of us are to go out in a *chasse* squadron and as there are 14 of us who have been trained in chasse, we wonder who the fortunate ones will be.

June 24

Bad weather. Bunny Merz and I secured a Springfield Rifle & Automatic and went on a wild boar hunt in the nearby forest which is very dense and wild. Although we saw a great many tracks and thoroughly scratched ourselves with brambles we encountered no boars. Perhaps it's just as well as said boars are reputed to be mighty ferocious. A stud poker game served to make the evening pass without much trouble.

June 25

This a.m. at about 8 o'clock we were suddenly awakened by a great crash. An aeroplane had fallen on the hill some three hundred yards from us and Hathaway and Maynor, who were just going out on a patrol, were killed. Hath died instantly and Maynor shortly after being rushed to the hospital at Toul. This is our first casualty in the 90th and goes damned hard. His motor pooped and he *verried* into the ground. The machine was a complete mass of broken wire and steel. Hath is the second of Section 17 to get bumped off.

At three p.m. they notified us that the fellows were to be buried and we rushed around for cars to get down in. We finally arrived and I acted as a pallbearer for Hath. He was buried in the cemetery north of Toul alongside of Lufbury and the rest of our men. During the ceremony, we had a machine fly over the grave and the exercises were read by two army chaplains. Went to a very

South Meuse Diary Locales

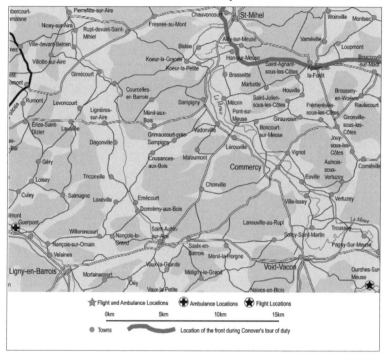

good concert given by the French in the R.C. Hut in the evening.

June 26

Walden & I flew over the lines on a reconnaissance this morning while Pink Ellis flew above us as protection. We were forced to go above the clouds on account of their being extremely low, but the visibility was good for the clouds were rather far apart. We received a welcome by our friends the Archies, but all shots fell short. Coming home Pink and I dived thru a white cloud bank together. Never have I seen a more beautiful sight than his machine silhouetted against a great fleecy cloud bank with his observer standing by his two machine guns. Then like a flash he shot into the mass, out of sight. We found each other about a minute later on the other side in exactly the same respective position.

Drove to Toul in the p.m. and placed wreathes on the graves of our friends. Then we all decided to drive to Nancy and, taking things in our own hands, "lit out." The party was very boisterous & a good time was had by all. We met a crowd from the 94th, 96th and 91st, and passed each other the latest dope on our respective squadrons. Arrived home in the "wee small hours" and after entertaining the boys against their will, turned in.

June 27

There are two English bombing squadrons near us. They are using DeHavilland 4's. This evening a D.H. landed on one aerodrome. The pilot showed his papers and said he was lost. They invited him to lunch & had a most sociable time. After his departure they learned that his papers were those of a man killed six months ago and thought the visitor returned to Germany, his native land. These planes are now marked with black squares as well as the circular insignia lest another visitor be received.

June 28

Booked to fly at dawn this morning but a heavy mist prevented. Day spent in usual way, swimming, reading, eating & talking.

June 29

Same as yesterday, life of indolence and *rien a faire.*

June 30

Was squadron officer of the day today & alternate on the "alert" but we managed to get in a baseball game in the afternoon and afterward a swim. Evening spent in turning off and putting on lights on account of hostile aircraft. The night was perfect.

July 1

Handed in my name for transfer to *chasse.* Some of the fellows are staying. Their chances for promotion are greater and the job is safer. After having flown a pursuit plane, yours truly will never stay in observation, but will be a damn fool as usual and take mine in a single seater Spad and *chercher les boches.*

July 2

Alternate on the alert again today, but the sector is so quiet that we had practically nothing to do. I flew the bi-plane Spad in the afternoon. It has not proved practical for observation purposes on account of the unreliability of the motor, but when she goes, she is certainly good. I had the time of my life flying and stunting a regular machine again.

July 3-to 12

Slipped up again—Well, on the evening of the Fourth we went to Toul where we danced with the fair sex from the hospitals. There were about five men to each nurse and the nurse was usually very sad, so we concentrated more on the punch than the dancing. Flew again the following day over the lines with the bi-plane Spad, we saw a couple of Huns but they did not give bat-tle. Bunny Merz and I spent the weekend in Nancy, where we had a mighty enjoyable time. I ran into Paul Behiens there and was sure glad to see him. We also met a large number of English aviators who are all A-1 fellows. Returned to Ourches July 7.

July 11, Ourches

The 96th bombing escadrille sent a formation of six planes led by Major Brown, over to bomb Koblenz. Five of them were forced to land in Germany, the sixth has not been heard from. This may take some of the damn foolishness out of the Americans. They have been forced to fly planes entirely unfit for this work and dis-carded by the French. Not a word of this has been allowed to get into the paper. If it were put in we might benefit by the experi-ence and our countrymen might lose some of their conceit and cockiness. A grand and glorious ending for the first American bombing squadron together with their commander.

Bob Browning, Henry Davis & several others with whom I went thru preliminary training were among them. The laugh is cer-tainly on them, and we intend to draw some cartoons represent-ing the first American bombing squadron dropping their machines & themselves on bocheland. We will fly over with these and drop them in Germany, where we will ask that they be forwarded to said prisoners.

Babe Ewing has been killed—hell.

July 12-to 23

The life out here has developed into very much of a sameness so that it is but a continual round of two days on and one off. The aerial activity in our sector has increased so that the excitement is a bit keener, but outside of a few of our planes being hit in the wings, nothing of moment has transpired. We swim in the Meuse at odd moments, dance with the nurses at Toul occasionally, and get a day off in Nancy once in a while—so life is very tolerable and the time passes quite pleasantly.

Johnny has gone on leave to Deauville and returned while Bunny and I are looking forward to a leave at the same place on the fifth of next month. Jerry Jerome was brought down in flames a few days ago, and Buck Freeman, Steve Brodie, and Hobie Baker crashed a boche over "no man's land." We have not been transferred as yet, but inasmuch as we have new planes, Salmsons, coming in, we are content to remain in this work a little longer as the experience is mighty good.

July 23-August 21

This is no longer a diary, but will have to be only a brief sketch of what I do from time to time. All conditions have become so common place that it is impossible to write with any degree of interest.

Life in the squadron continued as usual, we flew on our regular missions over the lines, had some interesting experiences and other hey day. No tremendously exciting incidents transpired.

WWI Events Second Half of 1918

1918

July   Germans strike across Marne in Second Battle of the Marne, the fifth and last attack of their Spring Offensive. Allies counterattack southwest of Marne. Germans retreat.

Aug.   French retake Soissans. Allied forces attack at Amiens and along much of the western front. Germans forced back to the Hindenburg Line.

Sept.   American and French attack Germans in St. Mihiel Offensive, restoring St. Mihiel to France and straightening Allied lines in the salient. Meuse-Argon Offensive launched a few days later. Germans fall back under continued American and French pres sure which is to continue until Armistice. After route of Balkan forces at Valdar, war in Balkans ends with Allied-Bulgarian armistice. British breach Hindenburg Line. Belgians regain Ypres

Oct.   Kaiser Wilheim II appoints Max von Baden Chancellor of Germany. Ludendorff forced to resign. Allied forces defeat Austrian army at Vittorio Venito in last battle of the war in Italy. After signing an armistice with the Allies, Turkey quits war.

Nov.   Hostilities end between Austro-Hungary and Hungary. British enter Mons, French take Rethel and Americans reach Sedan. Ebert replaces von Baden as Chancellor. Kaiser leaves Germany. **On November 11: General armistice signed by Allies and Germany. Hostilities cease.** German fleet surrenders to British. Kaiser Wilheim II abdicates. Poland and Yugoslavia declared sovereign states.

Dec.   Allies enter new German Republic.

Bar-le-Duc Area Locales

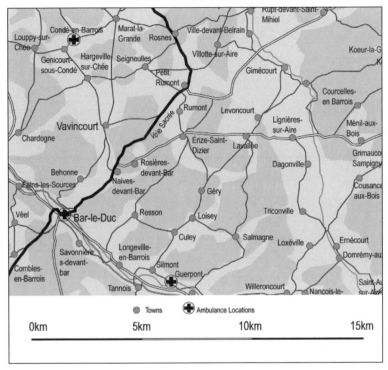

however.

Bunny Merz and I left the front August 2 for Deauville, where we spent seven days leave. Certainly had a hell of a good time. We swam, went horseback riding, automobile trips, met some very fine people and enjoyed ourselves thoroughly.

August 29

There is ever-increasing activity in our sector. American guns, supplies, munitions, and everything to do with war are being poured in. All of our air force has been moved up, and our chasse squadrons are restricted to patrols on our side only. Everything points to an all-American attack in the near future, and everyone in France is speculating upon it. The topography of the country to be taken is of the most difficult, however, and everyone wonders if it will be worth the price.

We are working very hard and have taken photographs of all the boche lines. Yesterday I spent four hours over bocheland taking photographs of their defenses and I am booked for the same work tomorrow.

I gave myself quite a thrill today that I won't forget for some time. The boche brought down three of our balloons so Hendricks, my observer, and I decided to try our luck on theirs. This is practically an impossible task in a two seater, but we thought we would try it anyway. So we loaded up with incendiaries, climbed up over the clouds and went over Germany. Our task was made extremely difficult, however, as the clouds were so thick that we could find no opening in them & had to go by guesswork and compass. Finally, when I thought we were about five kilometers in, I dived thru the clouds and came out over a boche hospital. No balloons were in sight, however, and we were forced to descend to 1200 meters to see the country.

There I received the thrill of my life, for nowhere were there signs of trenches, the sun was invisible, and my compass was whirling hopelessly. I therefore had to guess our direction & opened the throttle wide. Visions of landing in Germany, of being brought down, for at that height our position was hopeless, and a thousand similar thoughts flashed through my brain. However, luck was with us, and we had apparently done such a foolhardy thing that no one had suspected us. We passed over trucks and camions and could almost distinguish the Huns below us. Finally after what seemed like an age, I sighted the boche trenches dead ahead. Never have I seen a more welcome sight. Over we went with a black boche barrage popping around us and returned to report no German balloons up, to thank our stars that we were not in bocheland, and to wonder how we got back. After consulting a map, we learned that we had been some 15 to 20 kilometers deep in Hunland.

September 9

Things are certainly picking up. All night long we hear the rumble of caissons and the tramp of troops as they are being moved up to the lines. Every morning we have meetings in which we discuss the work to come and how best to accomplish it. A French captain of aviation lectures to us and answers the innumerable questions shot at him. Tanks of all sizes have been moved up, and their crews camouflaged under the insignia of other branches.

This morning we were told that we were to work in conjunction with the 42nd Division, which is to bear the brunt of the attack, and our work will carry us down over the troops within 300 meters of the ground. We will have to fly between the boche and American barrage dodging the trajectories of solid shells and

September 1918. Harvey Conover and his observer provide infantry liaison in the Verdun and St. Mihiel sectors in his #4 Salmson 2A2 of the 90th Aero Squadron.

"Sing" to afford as poor a target as possible for the boche machine gunners on the ground. This is by far the most dangerous work in all aviation so everyone is wondering who of us will be bumped off. However, everyone is also very anxious to get into it and see the most wonderful spectacle in the world–that of charging troops & tanks immediately below you.

The show is scheduled to commence in about two days, but the rain, which is now driving down, may delay it for several days. Everyone is keyed up to the highest pitch for upon this attack depends our success in the future to a great extent. It is the first all-American scrap and the entire world is talking about it. Our troops are greatly handicapped by their greenness and the physiography alone of the country to be taken creates a wonderful stronghold, yet we <u>must</u> obtain results at any cost. Our aviation, and we have a goodly number of squadrons in this sector, is pitifully green. The large majority of our airmen have never had a scrap, and a great many have never flown over the lines.

September 12-13-14

The "D" day was Sept. 12th the "H" hour was 5 a.m., and such a day as we had. Low flying clouds, a fine driving rain, damp, cutting, disagreeable. The barrage opened up at one a.m. At daybreak I took off and shot over the forest in back of our lines. Thousands of guns flashed out of the woods, doubly plain because of the low black clouds. Over we went dodging in and out of the mist until below us we could see our troops and tanks advancing. The bursting shells banged under us, and others on their way zipped by. It gradually became lighter and our troops could be made out more plainly, ever advancing behind our barrage, while the boche in their darker uniforms could be seen retreating. Great clouds of smoke issued from the villages behind the boche lines as they were hastily destroying all immovable supplies.

Back and forth we dodged in sharp turns and S turns to evade the machine gun fire from the ground while my observer was busy making notations of our progress below us. Finally we finished and started back thru our barrage to our lines. We passed over a multitude of flashing guns and our bus jumped up and down as solid shells shot by us churning up the air. However, we passed them without mishap and sent in our report as another one of our busses buzzed away to take up and continue the most exciting, spectacular and dangerous of all air work during an attack — "infantry liaison"

Our troops advanced 7 kilometers, took about 15,000 prisoners, and all in three days.

September 25, Verdun Sector

We have moved from the Toul sector and have now been in the Verdun sector for four days. We are jammed in leaky barracks, surrounded with mud. It has rained most efficiently. However, everybody's happy for we have a good and congenial bunch.

Tomorrow there is to be an attack from Reims to Verdun. We are taking care of the Verdun sector. It is to be the greatest offensive of the year. The plans of attack have been given out to us this evening. All have been busy making final preparations and working on their maps. Our dinner was a most hilarious one. A passerby would think we were on a month's vacation, and the singing was most enthusiastic, if not harmonious. Our morale is high, and I see no reason why we should not make good tomorrow.

September 29, Souilly

Well, our two divisions have successfully taken their objectives and conditions have quieted down fairly well again. We put down a barrage that tore the country to pieces, and our troops followed it up, taking everything before them. We were occupied chiefly with contact patrol, flying low just ahead of our barrage, noting the position of our troops, and that of the enemy. The sight is most magnificent: watching our men fighting their way from shell hole to shell hole, shells bursting all around you, and machine guns tack-tacking below you. It makes you want to yell to the men to give them hell, and it is more exciting than anything I have ever participated in.

There is a dark side to everything. However, and the bad part of this game is the large number of your friends who are killed. It is terrible to look back over the last year and remember your countless friends who have been killed, and it has now become so common that you accept the news of the death of a friend as you would the outcome of a baseball game. You say, "Oh is that so?" and straightway forget it. You can't help wondering, however, when your turn will come.

October 10, Verdun Sector

I have spent three days in Paris, most enjoyable avec ma femme and am back again. I was not supposed to go to that city but to some rest home in a nice pine atmosphere, so am now a bit out of favor with the festive Colonel.

Yesterday I went over to locate the enemy lines, and perceiving a boche officer on horseback dove on him giving him my machine gun. I don't know whether I got him or not, but his horse went tearing down the road as though the devil himself were after him. We then strafed the Huns in their trenches and returned home.

Today while making a reconnaissance we were chased by some fifteen Huns & each time we returned we were forced to dive back with full motor. Finally four got on my tail and Burger, my observer, opened up on them. His bullets, tracers & incendiaries, could be seen entering the nearest Fokker, and it was as pretty a sight as I have ever seen. Finally a cloud of smoke shot out of his engine and he went down in a nosedive. One of their bullets went thru my prop & several in my right wing. It was great sport & I enjoyed every minute of it.

October 28–November 28

Several things have happened since I have turned to this record, and I am now on board the S.S.Sierra, homeward bound, but as to the cause of this rather ignominious return via hospital ship, I must look back one month and a day.

Work had been going along in the Verdun sector at a truly terrific rate. Attacks had become an everyday affair, fights commonplace, and two of our men, Broomfield, and Cutter killed. Everyone is thoroughly fed up, his nerves on edge, owing to the fact that no leaves are obtainable. Half of our outfit has dysentery so badly, or is so stale that they cannot fly. The rest of us are doing the work, and we are certainly busy.

On the afternoon of October 27th Burger, my observer, and I left the aerodrome to do a contact patrol with our infantry on the right bank of the Meuse, who were to attack at 4 p.m. We found our barrage rather light and in spite of our many signals, no panels appeared. We were forced to descend and fly just above the treetops in order to locate the position of our troops, and we found them stopped by a murderous machine gun fire. We therefore began diving on these nests and had a great time shooting the pigs until, while I was in a low right hand bank, I was surprised by a crash. My left leg flew off the rudder and my goggles were covered with blood. The cockpit filled with smoke, and we started to spin for earth. It happened so quickly that surprise held me motionless for a second. However, I managed to get her out just above the earth and to poop over to our side. I landed just behind our trenches between two rows of barbwire near the village of Consenvoye. The bus stopped rolling about two feet behind a shell hole, and I had miraculously landed on the only smooth place north of Verdun.

Next I climbed, or rather fell, out on my good leg, and as my knee was intensely painful, gave up the next five minutes to cursing while Burger cut my pants off the wound. I found three rather large holes and many small ones, but none of them was

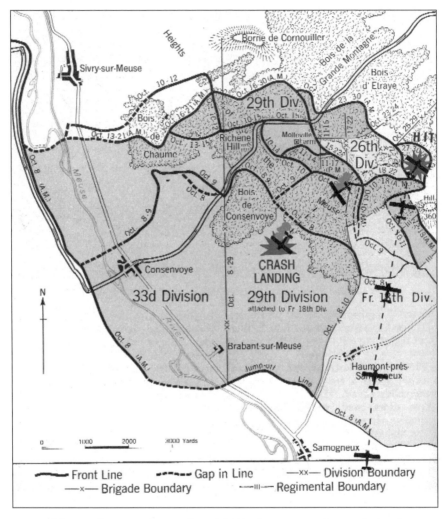

Front Line ▪▪▪▪▪ Gap in Line —xx— Division Boundary
—x— Brigade Boundary ▪▪▪ⅢⅠ▪▪▪ Regimental Boundary

visible on the outside, and as I picked out one piece of metal, which had not penetrated as deeply as the others, I was forced to conclude that my leg was well filled with steel. Two French

stretcher bearers arrived and bound up my leg as well as possible, but not without the loss of a great deal of blood. Next came
a stretcher ride of about three kilometers while I smoked inces-
santly and shivered as with the ague. I managed to quench my
thirst from a canteen of pinard but cannot state that the trip was
pleasurable.

After bumping along in this fashion, we finally reached a car
bound away from the lines and I was lifted into the back seat and
covered with blankets, in spite of which I could not get warm.
After three hours of crawling over shell-marked roads past batteries in action, troops moving up, and supply trains, we reached
Verdun and drove up to the citadel, where I was carried inside
and deposited on a dirty cot. Another wait of an hour, which
seemed like a day, and I was put in a Ford ambulance and driv-
en to a field hospital. Here I received a cup of hot chocolate and
a shot of anti-tetanus. I was somewhat worried about blood poi-
soning by this time, and asked to be operated upon as soon as
possible but learned that I had another trip before me before I
could have the pleasure of being cut up so I was loaded into
another ambulance along with three other wounded and jostled
along the road for another hour. The man above me spent his
breath groaning, and the one beside me vomiting while I
improved my time with the worst words I could think of.

We finally arrived at the hospital at Souilly, and I was clothed in
damp pajamas and placed between cold sheets. I shivered and
trembled and could not seem to get warm on account of loss of
blood. Next I was trundled upon another stretcher and carried

into the operating room. Here I was placed at the end of a row of about fifteen stretchers, covered with a dirty blanket, and left to await my turn. A suffocating odor of ether permeated the room, and doctors and nurses were busy administering anesthetic and operating at the tables about me. Men struggled as they went under the ether, lay prone and stiff while they were being cut open, and others talked drunkenly as they came out from under it. The man on the stretcher beside me, whose labored breathing I had been semi-conscious of, suddenly jumped, gasped, and lay still again. Then he gradually stiffened and was carried away to the morgue.

Finally I was again lifted up and taken into the Xray room, where I was speedily placed upon a table and examined. The report was snapped out in purely technical terms, meaning nothing to me except the presence of many foreign bodies in knee joint. Upon asking the operator, I was told that my knee was well filled with pieces of metal, and I would probably have a stiff knee from that date.

Again I was placed on a stretcher, and this time placed at the foot of the stretcher cases to be operated upon. I was now becoming very impatient as the idea of infection had been constantly in my mind, and I did not relish the idea of losing a leg on account of a delay that could be averted. Therefore, I talked with one of the doctors and asked that I be operated upon as soon as possible. He rushed me ahead of four or five men and at 2:30 a.m. I was lying upon the operating table. A surgeon began to talk to me, and I told him what I had in my knee and asked as a special favor that

he get it out. Next came a dulling of the sensibilities, then a
thump-bang-bang and I was tossing about in a black nightmare.

I awoke feeling a bit dizzy but intoxicated and began to kid the

*Aboard the SS Sierra. Conover shown between Lt. Sanford
Bauer and the "Fighting Chaplain" Roy Jenney. All were fea-
tured in Chicago Tribune article in December 1918*

nurse. She was not to be kidded, however, and was as sour an individual as I have ever seen. Much to my relief, she was soon replaced by the lay nurse, a more pleasant individual. I then had them call up Johnny at the aerodrome, and he met me with my suitcase as they loaded me on the train bound for the base hospital at Bordeaux. The effects of the ether now began to make themselves apparent to me, and I felt particularly rotten. I was placed in the middle tier of bunks just over the wheels, and the splint, which encased my leg, tied to the foot of the berth. The train started with a bump, and we began to crawl for Bordeaux. The trip was a nightmare. Bump, bump, bump, jerk, and we would stop then start, then stop again, and each jolt made my leg feel as though it was burning up. A man across from me groaned continually, and the entire convoy reminded me of Dante's inferno. Finally, after almost 48 hours of this pleasure, we arrived at Base Hospital 114 and just before the dawn I was unloaded and placed in a bed in Ward 11.

On account of lack of space I was put in the "dead room" and when morning arrived, a crowd of fellows came in and gathered around my bed. The day nurse, an attractive girl (something rare among A.E.F. nurses) came in and started to dress my leg. Then the fun started--"What's your name and rank? Who do you want us to notify?" asked one. "Better amputate," says another. "He'll never get well. You may be well when you come in, but they will carry you out stiff." Such encouraging comments were shot at me from all sides, and for a moment I did not know just what to think. Then I learned that it is the custom to stand around all dressings and pass as many pessimistic remarks as possible. The next four or five days were more or less uncomfortable. I had to be given something every night to make me sleep. Another X-ray was taken, and the plate showed many particles still unremoved, and a piece of bone chipped off. They decided to remove the splint, however, and I was soon comparatively comfortable and well on the road to recovery.

Ward 11 contained 60 beds all filled, and one nurse had to take care of 60 dressings daily, some of them very severe. Two stoves served as heating apparatus, and the whole place reeked with lack of proper and sufficient help. A bed patient would not be given a bath, and some went as long as four months without one. The ward was never thoroughly clean as a careless sweeping was all it ever received, and that once a day.

The patients, however, were wonderful, and in spite of the great amount of suffering, one seldom heard a groan or a complaint. The ward was never quiet as someone was always singing, kidding the nurse, or someone with a bad wound raising hell generally. There was always a goodly number of fellows well advanced on the road to recovery who could get around and they furnished amusement for those less fortunate ones who were still forced to remain in bed. I was soon up and around on crutches and made several trips to Bordeaux when they finally, against my wishes, sent me home.

I greatly improved while on the boat in spite of unusually rough weather, and before we landed I was able to get around with the aid of a cane only and had full use of my knee.

The SS Sierra, on which we returned, was a small tub of only

10,000 tons. Before the war it had been used as a fruit carrier on the Pacific, and was entirely unfit for Atlantic travel. Seventeen hundred wounded soldiers and fifty wounded officers were crowded on her, and many were forced to sleep on deck on account of the lack of space and the bad air in the hold. For three days, a gale averaging 55-60 miles an hour threw us around unmercifully, and we were barely able to hold steerageway against it. She pounded terribly and finally several of the steel plates in her bow were loosened allowing great quantities of water to rush in. All pumps were manned, and for some time no headway was made against the inrush, but finally the hole was partially filled with concrete, and she was again under control. This gave our Naval Officers, who do not seem to be acquainted with danger, quite a scare, and they told us of the episode with drawn faces. They live a life of luxury, have eggs for breakfast every morning, and a great many of them receive more attention than they had at home. Meanwhile the risks they run are infinitesimal compared to those of the army.

We arrived at New York harbor the morning of Dec. 9, and about eight o'clock we steamed in. Then every whistle in port opened up in our honor, and midst the din men, women, and children on packed ferryboats yelled and waved to us. A fireboat ran alongside, and with all streams flowing escorted us in. It was one of the greatest sights I have ever witnessed, this homecoming and welcome after two years in a foreign land.

The Red Cross women were lined up at the dock waving flags, and a band played for us.

Then came the work of getting us off the boat and to a hospital ten miles distant. All day long we stood around on account of their inefficient delay. We finally arrived at the hospital in the evening, extremely irritated. Then when the hospital officials wanted to sterilize our clothing, which would of course ruin it, and treated us like a species of wild beast, we rose up in arms, and told them to go to hell. There was a great uproar, but we finally agreed to let them examine us for cooties, which to their great disgust, they did not find. We then all turned in utterly tired out and disgusted.

The following day I went down to N.Y. City where I had a most enjoyable afternoon and returned at about 9 p.m. Went to bed feeling fine but awoke at 3 a.m. with chills, fever, and sick to my stomach. The next four days were perfectly disgusting. My trouble proved to be an infection and my leg turned red down to my ankle. I couldn't eat & continually burned and felt cold. The doctors thought that I would surely pass out, but I managed to fool them and pulled through.

Of the next month there is little to tell. The Folks came down worried stiff and stayed about a week. I have spent my time lying in bed cursing everything in the world and taking morphine to make me sleep at night. They say pain purifies the recipient, but they're all wrong. Am now able to stagger around on crutches and will get that knee well if I break my neck doing it. In spite of the doctors instead of because of them.

Friends killed in the EUROPEAN WAR 1917-1918.

In chronological order showing place of death.

René Huré, July 17, 1917 – Near Verdun

A young Frenchman with whom we became very well acquainted during the stay of his regiment in Jubécourt. He was a very high-class fellow, well educated, & had lived for some time in England. He had entered the war at the start as a Private, and had worked up to the rank of an Aspirant. He was to have been promoted to a Lieutenant after the attack. All of us in Section 17 had become very much attached to him and will always hold his name in honor.

A. Courtney Campbell, Oct. 3, 1917 – French Front

I became well acquainted with Codie at White Lake, Michigan, and first met him at the christening of an early Revonoc. He was a fellow who possessed a great spirit of adventure and was often thought a bit wild by conservative parents. I remember in particular one evening spent with him at Montague when we returned full speed in his hydroplane. He joined the Ambulance about four months before I did and transferred into the American Escadrille of the French army. While at the front he distinguished himself by landing with one plane completely shattered. I saw him in Paris, not more than a week before his death. He was in to see Dr. Gros about transferring into the American Army. The report says that he was brought down while encountering several boche planes. Codie died as he has always lived--game.

Earnest Leach, Jan. 20, 1918 – Issoudun

Leach is, or rather was, a very quiet and retiring young fellow who always acted very much the part of a gentleman. He was formerly an ambulance man, but when the U.S. declared war, he entered our aviation service. I became acquainted with him in the flying school at Tours, where he finished satisfactorily and went to Issoudun for the aerobatics and finishing work. While flying in a 15-meter Nieuport, he went into a wing slip at 100 meters & crashed to earth, mangled almost beyond recognition. Leach is the first of our crowd to go, and it will be long before we forget him.

A.H. Wilson, February 23, 1918 – Issoudun

"A.H." as we always called him, was one of the finest fellows I have ever known. Although not inclined toward athletics, he was a good sport and a mixer. He was a musical genius playing classical music on the piano with perfect expression and technique. Morally he was perfect and a gentleman through and through. While making his second *tour de piece* in the 18 meters, he fell into a nosedive on his turn and crashed to earth being killed instantly. "A.H." leaves us all thinking of him as one of the very best that they have in this world.

George Phillipeatroux, February 25, 1918 – Issoudun

Phil stood about 6 feet 2 in his stocking feet, as an amateur comedian he had no peer, and he was as likeable a fellow as they make them. He had only finished his instruction at this school a few days ago, but because he was one of the best flyers that we have ever had, he was given the position as tester vacated by Kiekland, a Frenchman who was killed a short time ago. Phil, while flying a 15 at the height of 2000 ft. was seen to go into a *verrie* and he crashed to the ground on the "Reveller" field. He is the second to go in two days, and the entire camp is sad and gloomy.

"Buts" Butler, March 14, 1918 – Tours

"Buts" was in my flying class at Tours and finished his brevet tests shortly after I. He was a rather steady, quiet fellow who tried diligently to learn French and to better himself as much as possible in his life in this country. He crashed to earth on a turn in an 18-meter and died a few days after.

Jewell White, March 20, 1918 – Cazaux

"Whitie" hailed from Chicago and was a sure-enough live wire. He went thru Tours a little ahead of me, but I became well acquainted with him down here. He was a good flyer and damned good company. While practicing gunnery at Cazo his plane collapsed and we lost "Whitie," but we won't forget him.

Leslie Chandler, March 27, 1918 – Texas

"Les" was a fellow Hinsdalian somewhat younger than I so altho I saw him very often at home, I was never very well acquainted with him. He was killed in an accident while instructing in flying at an aviation field in Texas.

"Cop" Copley, April 1918 – Tours

While at Cazaux I learned that "Cop" had left us. He is the second of my original double control class at Tours to go. He was also a great friend of Butler, being very much like him in that he was serious, steady and quiet. He was testing and it was the old story of a *verrie* stopped at the ground that killed him.

Harry Colburn, May 10, 1918 – Issoudun

Harry went as far as Field 7 with me then took a position as instructor at Field 5. He was killed this morning while flying alone, and no one knows what happened. Harry was a mighty fine fellow and a live wire.

Stewart Freeman, May 10, 1918 – Issoudun

Stew was killed last night. He was struck by a train near here. Harry Webb, in trying to save him, had his hand taken off. It seems it never rains without pouring.

Dick Blodgett, May 18, 1918 – Toul

Dick was located near Toul, which is not far from Amanty.

While flying over the lines, he evidently was in combat for while returning to his aerodrome at a height of only 200 meters, his machine was seen to fall. A bullet hole was found in his lung. Dick went through Tours a little ahead of me but slept near me while there. Dick was quite a boy.

Raoul Lufbury, May 19, 1918 – Front

I met Luf while on the train for the front. He had 18 official boche to his credit and was the best man in the Lafayette. He transferred to the American Army when U.S. entered was made a Major. In spite of this, however, he was the most popular man among us for he remained a good fellow. When he returned to his escadrille the alarm was given and he went up with several others to attack a boche. While climbing on him he was shot from under the Hun tail, which proved to be a three seater. His plane caught on fire and when at a height of about 2000 meters he jumped from his plane. We have lost a great aviator & a white man, but revenge will come.

John Mitchell, May 27, 1918 – near Toul

John went to the U. of Wisconsin the same time I did, and was one of my very good friends. He was a mighty fine fellow and well liked by everyone. He came over with the first ground school crowd and received his training in France. John was killed while flying with the 95th, which was stationed near Toul which is 35 kilometers from Amanty.

Don Asa Bigelow, June 3, 1918 – near Paris

Don is the first member of Section 17 to be killed. He came over with me, I was with him at the front, we enlisted at the same time in Paris, and trained together so I knew him very very well. He was a man who improved upon acquaintance, as fine a boy as I have ever known. He was occupied in ferry work in Paris until chasse planes should arrive and was killed in a fall with a Sopwith. Well, these post mortems are becoming a daily occurrence but I will say that I miss Don more than anyone so far.

E. Trafton Hathaway, June 25, 1918 – Ourches

Hath came over to France with me, we were in Ambulance Section 17 together, enlisted in U.S. Air Service at Paris and we were together at Tours. He did not go thru Issoudun with me, and we were separated until some three weeks ago when he joined the 90th. He crashed to earth at 8:00 a.m. while leaving for the front on a mission. He is he second of our original bunch who left the section for the aviation to be killed.

Elbridge W. Maynor, June 25, 1918 – Ourches

Maynor joined our squadron as an observer a short time ago, and was very well liked by all. He was killed with Hathaway.

Yale Squire, July 2, 1918 – France

News has come to me that Yale, who has been acting as a Caudron instructor, has been killed. He started training with me at Tours and was for awhile in my double control class. He was tall raw-boned fellow, and had great difficulty in learning how to fly. A better hearted fellow never lived, however. He was well-liked by everyone.

Mac Weddell, July 3, 1918 – off France

Mac was an old acquaintance from Hinsdale and a great boy. He was one of the first U.S. Navy aviators in France and considered one of the best. He did patrol duty from San Bajare looking for subs. While coming in from a patrol a wing fell off his plane and he crashed. Both Mac & his observer were killed.

Babe Ewing, July 6, 1918 – France

Babe hailed from Baltimore and was a peach. He, Bunny Merz & I had some of the best times in the world together at Issoudun, and I thought the world and all of Babe. He was always full of pep, and an ideal man for any occasion. When we were sent to the front, fate decreed that he should be put on a ferry job and he flew a plane out to us only a week ago, and we all had a great reunion. While flying into a field today, however, he hit a wire with his tail and crashed. We all will miss Babe like the devil.

Jerry Jerome, July 13, 1918 – Front

Jerry and I went thru Tours together. He was a quiet, retiring, chap, a good artist who liked to make verses. He was brought down in flames while patrolling the Nancy sector with a French Escadrille.

Kasper Kiekland, July 15, 1918 – Tours

Kasper trained with me at Issoudun but afterward went to Tours to instruct. He was an independent person and very good company. He was killed in a flying accident at Tours.

David Davidson, July 20, 1918 – Front

Davie went thru flying school with me and hailed from California. He was sent out with the French and brought down in flames in a fight.

Others Missing, Killed, or Taken Prisoner

Buck Freeman (prisoner)	Bob Converse
Steve Brodie	Quentin Roosevelt
Pep Foster (prisoner)	Alan Nutt
Chas. Drew	Lawrence Layton
Art Kimber	Tommie Thompson.
Dave Putnam (killed)	Pat Anderson
"General" Strauch	John Tyler
Roger Chapin (prisoner)	Maurice Manier
Glen Richardson	Jerrey Stivers
Frank West	Hugh Boomfield
Ed Cutter	Red Kahle

Ben Boldt C.A. Brodie

Pat Patterson Farnie Farnsworth

Nov. 11, 1918

The sun is shining brightly

O'er all of Northern France

The frightful war is over

And joy and cheer entrance

.

There's singing and there's laughter

The populace is gay

For this is our great victory

And this is our great day

But there are many soldiers

Who brought this victory

Who do not cheer, who do not sing

Nor join the revelry

Never will they tell of deeds

Around the family hearth

Never will they have the praise

Balm to the tired hearts

So let us not forget the men

Who gave up most of all

They now lie stiff & cold in France

Under her soils pall

For better men than you or I

Were called while young & gay

To lose their lives and die for us

Do not forget them — pray!

A Soldier's Toast

Here's a toast to the girl

Who true would stay

And marries at home

An embusque

Here's a toast to the damsels

To all of us dear

Who are with our brave men

Who have chosen the rear

We can sit, we can dream,

Of our comrades gone,

We can fight, we can die

With a curse or a song

And those who are spared

When the bells are rung

Will return, but not sing

Of the deeds they've done.

For they know what it is

To suffer and fear

The brave tales will come

From those in the rear.   - -Kipling

Harvey Conover receives Distinguished Service Cross at ceremony in Long Island, NY. December 1918.

AFTERWARDS

AFTERWARDS

Dad vowed in the last entry of his wartime diary to "get that knee well if I break my neck doing it." He cast off his crutches soon after leaving the Veteran's hospital. He used a cane for a short time, and for many years walked with a slight limp.

There were joyous shouts of welcome when he came through the door of his family home in Hinsdale, Ill. He wore the Distinguished Service Cross, Croix de Guerre, and Aero Club Medal of Honor "for extraordinary heroism." His father, mother, older sister Polly, younger brothers George and Dick, along with many friends were all there to greet him. They echoed the euphoric belief of the whole country that their brave men had won "the war to end all wars" and that there would be no more fighting, and no more killing.

Despite diary entries stating that he would never settle down, marry, and live in the suburbs, he did just that. Within a year of his arriving home, a mutual friend introduced him to Sarah Dorothy Jobson who lived in the nearby suburb of La Grange. They dated for several months. She had fallen in love with him as soon as she saw him. He was a big man: handsome, six feet tall with broad shoulders, a ready wit and a booming laugh. She once confided to me, "I always get a thrill when he enters the room."

Years later, I asked Mom about their courtship. She told me, "We were on a double date riding in the back seat of a friend's car. Our friend drove around a curve too fast, the car tipped over. Dad fell on top of me, and we had a difficult time extricating ourselves from the car. Luckily we were not hurt, and that evening he asked me to marry him."

Mom was beautiful, vivacious, and intelligent. Dad said in his diary that he admired the French women because they were so "full of pep." Webster defines pep as "brisk energy or initiative and high spirits." While Dad may have had more in mind when he used the word in the diary, Mother perfectly met Webster's definition. Although Mom and Dad differed in many ways, they made a lasting impression on everyone they met. Married on June 23, 1920, their marriage lasted the rest of their lives.

Mom told me that before they were married they decided that they would not have children for five years. Within that time span, they had three: my sister Dorothy Anne in 1921, I arrived a year and a half later, and my brother Harvey Conover, Jr., in 1925. My younger brother, Larry, was born five years later.

Dad started his business career in Chicago selling advertising space for the publishing firm A.W. Shaw Co. From 1921 to 1927, he rose from salesman to western manager, vice president, and president of the Engineering Magazine Co. In 1922, the company transferred him to New York City. After living in the city for a short time, the family moved to a house in Larchmont, New York, a bedroom community for New York, just twenty miles North of the city.

Dad traveled a lot, but spent most weekends at home. He worked hard and still made time for his family. We spent many evenings playing Ping-Pong. He hit the ball with gusto, slamming his paddle against the table when he missed a shot.

We loved to gather around the piano and sing. Mom played the piano and often Dad added his booming bass voice. I remember the parties at our little yellow house in Larchmont. It was during Prohibition, but somehow Dad and his friends were able to get liquor. Couples brought their own bottle to parties.

Unfortunately, as the years went by, Dad's drinking became a problem. During my teenage years, I sometimes hesitated to invite friends home with me, fearing he might be drinking. One Christmas Eve Dad came home from a company party and tipped over the Christmas tree, which we had just finished trimming. Many of the lights and ornaments were broken. Those were difficult years for the family, especially for my mother. When he finally recognized the problems his drinking was causing, both in his business and at home, Dad gave it up cold turkey. A few years later, when he developed a terrible cough, he stopped smoking the same way.

When I was sixteen we moved from Larchmont to the neighboring town of Mamaroneck. Mother and Dad built a house about 25 feet above the water on a spit of land jutting out into Larchmont Harbor on Long Island Sound. It was a beautiful spot surrounded by water and magnificent views, a gathering spot for family and friends. There was something for each generation: swimming, boating, and laughter. Several friends and relatives anchored their boats off our dock. We ate many meals on the terrace in the backyard during the warm months. Many years Mom and Dad hosted a large clam bake with lobsters, clams, and all the trimmings. Across the road from our front yard lay a lovely sandy beach where we picnicked and swam.

In 1927 Dad and his long-time friend, Bud Mast, founded their own company, the Conover-Mast Publishing Company. The new company started with the publication of one magazine, *Mill and Factory*. By his death in 1958, the company published seven successful magazines. Each new magazine reflected his genuine belief that it would provide a valuable resource to the industry involved. His partner Bud Mast described Dad as a "many-sided man, a prodigious worker with the irresistible drive of a 500 horsepower bulldozer. Moreover, he was a perfectionist. Nothing was ever just 'good enough'. He stood for perfection in everything he did. If you met Harvey once, you never forgot him. It was impossible for him to make a merely mild impression-whether his first contact was with a minister or a shoeshine man, it was an uninsulated person-to-person meeting."

When World War II came, Dad again sought ways to contribute to the war effort. He believed the concept of service was important, both to the country and to the business world. He conceived the idea of applying collective American industrial know-how to the national task of producing the equipment needed for waging war. He promptly went to Washington to sell Donald Nelson, chairman of the War Production Board, on a know-how handbook that could help millions of newcomers in war plants learn how to use and maintain their tools and equipment. Nelson bought the idea, and Dad walked out with official entrée to every equipment manufacturer in America.

He and other representatives from Conover-Mast called on manufacturers all over the country asking how they operated and maintained their factory machinery. The data gathered was checked with manufacturers with similar equipment. The result: a widely-used 790 page handbook for war plants. It was published as a special issue of *Mill & Factory*.

The job was so good that the British asked him to make the same kind of information available in their factories. He worked in England three months, delighted to be back in action. He set up a program for continuous exchange of information through correspondence and missions.

At the request of the U.S.Navy, Dad took on the job of reporting on the aircraft maintenance operations of the Navy. A letter, dated February 25, 1945 to my brother, Harv, a Midshipman at Annapolis at the time, gives a detailed report of his adventures during this assignment. A quote from this letter says, "The idea behind it is to attempt to describe the vital part played by the men who keep 'em flying. These birds work like the devil. They undergo great hardship in forward areas. They are often subjected to enemy bombing attacks. The success of every mission is completely dependent upon their work and skill. Yet they are never in the public eye and receive no credit for the vital part they play on every strike against the enemy. In short, they are the guards and tackles who make the holes for the back-field, who make the headlines. So—in order to obtain this material it has been necessary to visit one of each of the operations." (Dad's entire letter is included in the Appendix}

Dad visited and analyzed the Navy operations on the East and West Coasts and the Pacific Islands. Among his experiences was a catapult take-off from an aircraft carrier. He also accompanied the crew of a PB4Y Liberator on a combat mission across the China Sea. During this mission, the plane dropped bombs and sank a small Japanese cargo ship. He thus became one of the relatively few people who flew on combat missions in both World Wars. A complete issue of Conover-Mast's publication, *Aviation Maintenance and Operations*, was devoted to his report. The Navy reprinted 250,000 copies and made it available to all its Naval Aviation ground forces.

Dad's entry in his diary on October 1, 1917 states, "Took my first flight today and sure was crazy about it. I really believe that I enjoy flying more than sailing and that is going some." After World War I, sailing became Dad's favorite way of relaxing when he was not working.

Soon after the family moved to the East Coast, he joined the Larchmont Yacht Club, a famous sailing mecca, and bought a sailboat. This was the first of several boats, countless races, and many cruises. He encouraged my sister, brothers and me to take sailing lessons. Sailing answered both his need for competition and adventure. Besides competing in races up and down Long Island Sound, he raced from Miami to Nassau, from Newport to Bermuda, around the Fastnet Rock off the Irish coast, and many other places.

His last four boats were named Revonoc; (Conover spelled backwards). With his Revonocs, he won 23 firsts, 14 seconds and six thirds in major races. Rated among the top dozen ocean-racing yachtsmen, he became Rear Commodore of the Larchmont Yacht Club, Commodore of the Cruising Club of America and Commodore of the North American Station of the Royal Swedish International Yacht Club.

*At family home in Mamaroneck 1946. L to R front: Frances(daughter),
Dorothy(wife), Dorothy Anne(daughter), Lynn(granddaughter), L to R
second row: Richard Gagney(son-in-law), Harvey, Jr.(son), Lawrence (son),
Charles Kingsley (son-in-law), and Harvey Conover*

For many years, Dad spent most of his sailing time racing, but as he grew older, he gradually gave up racing and spent
more time cruising on the boat. During his last years he spent six
weeks each winter sailing in Southern waters.

Our closest times as a family were our cruises together
on the Revonocs. Dad could relax and enjoy the challenge of
harnessing the wind to the sails of his boat. We all enjoyed working together to get the most speed out of the boat no matter what
the wind. We sailed to many harbors in Long Island Sound,
Maine, Cape Cod, Chesapeake Bay, Florida, and the Bahamas.

Dad loved to discover new places to sail. Among the
Southern ports Dad and Mom cruised were the Bahama Islands,
Jamaica, Cuba, and the Windward Islands. My parents always
cruised with family or friends aboard. His last boats were about
45 feet in length, yawl rigged and had auxiliary engines. The last
Revonoc was shoal draft, had an aluminum mast, roller reefing,
a diesel auxiliary engine, and an automatic pilot.

Dad was the captain. All those aboard had confidence in
him. Whether racing or cruising he made sure there were skilled
sailors aboard. He plotted the courses, studied the landfalls, the
currents and the charts, and Mother made sure that there were
ample supplies of food aboard.

*   *   *   *

On New Year's Day in 1958 the Coast Guard reported
the Revonoc overdue in Miami. Aboard were Dad, Mother, my
brother Larry and his wife Lori, and a friend of Larry's, Bill

Fluegelman. They were on the last leg of a two-week trip in the Bahama Islands, sailing overnight from the Florida Keys to Miami. Dad had checked with the Key West weather station before leaving the dock, the forecast was clear. However, some time in the middle of the night they were caught in what was reported to be one of the the the worst storms in the history of south Florida.

They were sailing in the Straits of Florida where the Gulf Stream flows north at speeds up to six knots. A high wind blowing against the stream creates huge waves and turbulent seas. It is a dangerous place for a small boat in a storm.

Navy, Coast Guard and Air Force planes were joined in the search by helicopters, a Navy blimp, and the big Coast Guard cutter Sebago. Civilian planes and vessels of the Cuban Navy and military aircraft also took part. For weeks, shores, reefs, islands and waters were combed in all directions. Six days after Revonoc was reported missing, her dinghy Revonoc Jr was found adrift off Jupiter Inlet, 80 miles north of Miami, its bow was stoved in.

All those aboard the Revonoc were skilled, experienced sailors. Mom had sailed with Dad for many years. She could handle the helm, trim the sheets, and serve efficiently on her watch. My brother Larry was a former president of the Intercollegiate Sailing Association and 1951 national champion of the 110 Class. He raced and cruised with Dad many times. Lori had sailed with Larry and was strong, alert, and able, as was Bill Fluegelman who had served aboard a Coast Guard cutter with Larry during the Korean War.

I can attest to Dad's skill and resourcefulness in dealing with sailing emergencies. My first husband and I were on board the previous Revonoc with the folks during an unexpected storm making a crossing between the Bahamas and Forida a year earlier. The wind gusted up to 65 knots. The waves were mountainous. We lowered all the sails, set the storm trysail, and hove to. The seas came aboard from well forward to clear aft of the cockpit. As the wind increased, the slide fastenings of the trysail broke loose one by one. I was at the helm and called Dad on deck. Dad acted quickly and confidently. On his orders we lowered the sail. He took the helm and quickly turned the boat so it was going before the wind. He then had us trail all the spare lines off the stern. These acted as a sea anchor and the boat steadied considerably. No more water came aboard, and we rode the waves like a sleigh ride. I remember Dad saying, "See, she's as steady as a church." We sailed with the wind with bare poles until the storm abated. Then we raised the sails, and tacked back to Fort Lauderdale a day late, but safe and sound.

*   *   *   *

There are many theories as to what happened. The newest Revonoc was only six months old, launched in June of 1957, designed by Sparkman & Stephens and built by Derecktor Boat Works in Mamaroneck. It had been tank tested under the highest specifications. Every step in her construction came under rigid scrutiny, and she had cruised enough to have shaken down the little details that always need a final touch.

However, something may have happened to the steering gear, or some other part of the boat. Perhaps one of the many freighters that traverse the Straits of Florida hit them. The seas were rough and the visibility poor. In heavy weather the ship's radar may not have been operating effectively, and the impact of collision with a sailboat might not have been felt by the crew of a larger vessel.

Another possibility is that at the height of the storm she may have been going before the wind with bare poles. Perhaps a large wave came aboard and she broached or pitch poled.

Many weeks passed before family and friends of those who were lost could accept that they were gone. The loss of so many loved ones left a large gap in many people's lives.

At the time of the accident my sister Dorothy and her husband and five children lived in Ohio. My brother Harv, who later became president of Conover Mast, and his wife were living in Chicago. His wife was pregnant with their fourth child.

My brother Larry and his wife Lori left two children; Mary Aileen, age two and a half, and Sarah Leslie, a year younger. My husband and I lived in Larchmont. Larry and Lori and their children lived nearby in Connecticut. We were close and had spent a lot of time with each other. When Larry and Lori were lost our children were eight and ten. It seemed natural to adopt the little girls. The children helped me to survive the tragedy. They are a treasured part of our family.

Dad said at the beginning of his diary that he was setting out in search of Adventure, which he believed to be "that most attractive phase in the lives of the human race." His full life indicates his attainment of this early goal. He was a firm and generous man, loved and admired by many. He achieved much success and was a true leader. He will live on in the memories of all whose lives he touched.

Frances Conover Church

Harvey Conover in Long Island Sound at helm of his last Revonoc *soon after its launching in 1957.*

Appendix

SOLDIERS HONORED BY PERSHING FOR HEROISM

(From Official U. S. Bulletin, Jan. 7, 1919)

The commander in chief, in the name of the President, has awarded the distinguished service cross to the following named officers and soldiers for the extraordinary heroism described after their names:

First Lieut. Harvey Conover, Air Service, pilot, 3d Observation Group. For extraordinary heroism in action near Consenvoye, France, October 27, 1918. Flying at an altitude of less than 50 meters over enemy artillery and machine guns, which were constantly firing on him, Lieut. Conover and his observer staked the American front lines and gave valuable information and assistance to the advancing infantry. Although suffering from two severe wounds, and with a seriously damaged plane, he delivered a harassing fire on six enemy machine gun nests which were checking the advance of the ground troops and successfully drove off the crews of four guns and silenced the other two. He then made a safe landing and forwarded his information to division headquarters before seeking medical aid.

Home address, L. . Conover, father, Hinsdale, Ill."

GENERAL HEAD QUARTERS

OF THE

FRENCH ARMIES OF THE EAST

GENERAL STAFF

Personnel Bureau
(Decorations)   ORDER No. 12.425 - "D." (EXTRACT)

      With the approval of the General Commanding the American Expeditionary Forces in France, the Marshal of France Commanding the French Armies of the East cites in Army Orders

·· ,

      Lieutenant Harvey CONOVER, Pilot in Squadron 90, U. S.

      "A Pilot of proved courage and daring. On October 8, 1918, he displayed soldierly qualities of the highest order in not allowing himself to be deflected from his military objective in spite of three successive attacks on him by enemy patrols. He succeeded in forcing down an enemy plane which fell disabled within its own lines, and, his aeroplane riddled with bullets, he returned with full and detailed information."

·· ·····

      At General Head Quarters, 19 December 1918.

             P E T A I N.

           Marshal of France,
      Commanding the French Armies of the East.

Feb. 25, 1945

Dear Harv:

Since returning I have become expert on the typewriter—-so to prove my cunning on this here device I will write you a letter forthwith.

Had a grand trip and enjoyed every minute of it. I'm also afraid that I'll have to admit that our stuffed shirt Navy is doing an excellent job. Now if you will get out your map of the Pacific I will give you a blow by blow account of my travels.—-

This particular job, as you may know, entails a description of the Navy's aircraft maintenance operations. The idea behind it is to attempt to describe the vital part played by men who keep 'em flying. These birds work like the devil. They undergo great hardship in forward areas. They are often subjected to enemy bombing attack. The success of every mission is completely dependent upon their work and skill. Yet they are never in the public eye and receive no credit for the vital part they play on every strike against the enemy. In short they are the guards and tackles who make the holes for the backfield, who make the headlines.

So—-in order to obtain this material it has been necessary to visit one of each of the operations.

To begin at the beginning, in November I went aboard one of our CVPs on a shake down and observed the operation of their flight deck and hangar deck gang—-the guys responsible for maintenance aboard a carrier. This job was done aboard the Randolph on Chesapeake Bay.

From the carrier I went to the Naval Air Station at Norfolk, Va., thence to a station at Atlantic City devoted to the training of carrier maintenance personnel, and from Atlantic City to Quonset, Mass., where there is a large sea plane base. This completed my coverage of the east coast, and I took a plane to San Diego. From San Diego I flew to Seattle, then back south to Port Huememe, some twenty-five miles north of Los Angeles, where they train forward area maintenance units. Back again to Dago where I boarded a CVE (jeep carrier to you) and accompanied them on a cruise devoted to the final training of a carrier pilot squadron. This was simply to be a check out, in which each pilot was to make eight satisfactory landings, then on catapult take off. It was planned to return within four days so I made a date to visit Port Huememe on the fifth and finish up that job. As luck would have it, however, when they had finished up with this squadron a dispatch was received which ordered them to remain at sea and train a squadron of night fighters. Consequently, because I had gotten the information I desired and because I wanted to keep my appointment at Port Huememe, I persuaded the Captain to let me fly in with one of the pilots of the squadron that had just completed its training-and therein lies a tale.

The take off was to be a catapult. I was to fly on a torpedo bomber, and my pilot was a swell guy who had the D.F.C. He had already put in six months at Midway and was training this new outfit. Well, I climbed into the bombers' seat aft, and my pilot took great pains to tell me what I should do on the catapult take off. There are, as you may know, two handles in front of the bombers' seat. It is very important that you lean forward and hold on to these handles on the catapult take off as the shock of jumping to some ninety miles an hour from a standing start within a few seconds is terrific. He concluded his instructions by telling me that the catapult officer would advise me when I should get set, so I relaxed and awaited instructions.

We taxied up to the bow of the ship and I then amused myself watching the airdales fasten the plane onto the catapult—then wham! All of a sudden there was an explosion, I was thrown back practically horizontal and was sure the plane had blown up into a mil-

lion pieces. They write about people recalling all of
the details of their youth when they are about to die
and now I know exactly what they mean. I covered each
and every moment of my fifty-two years, and no foolin!

Of course the catapult officer had simply forgotten to warn me and I had taken it sitting up.
Fortunately, I was completely relaxed, if I hadn't
been it would have been just too bad. Finally I came
to, and realized that I was still among the living and
that we were on our way to the shore, some three hundred miles distant. But this ain't all. When we
reached Port Huememe airfield my pilot pal started
stunting hell out of the plane, circled the field several times, and then, instead of landing flew to Los
Angeles. Here he again stunted the plane while I hung
on, and we finally landed. When we were on the ground
I learned that the landing gear wouldn't come down and
this accounted for the acrobatics. He was trying to
sweat out the landing gear and when unable to do so
decided that he'd prefer to crash on his home
field—hence the flight to L.A. However, fortunately
for both of us, he was able to sweat it out before
landing.

As soon as we got out of this crate, the pilot
turned to a Mech and asked for another. He was determined to get me to Port Huememe that evening, come
hell or high water! So we took off again and reached
our destination about sun-down—then what did we do but
blow a tire and do a ground loop.

Needless to say, I was delighted to get my feet
on terra-firma again, and was delighted in addition,
that the cycle of three near accidents had been completed.

From Port Huememe I flew to San Francisco in a
carrier dive bomber and after waiting a few days took
off from Alameda airport for Pearl Harbor. The flight
to Pearl was without incident, except that it was as
cold as the devil, and a strong head wind lengthened
the trip to fifteen and a half hours. Honolulu is

packed jammed. Sailors, marines and soldiers are so numerous that there isn't even room to walk on the sidewalks. All merchants, who are mostly Chinamen, at least with the exception of the large stores, are cleaning up. And in order to maintain a semblance of discipline there is a ten p.m. curfew and drinks are available only two hours each day. It's really so crowded that this is one restriction that everyone admits is essential.

Later - Your Maw seems to have become most social. She hauled me away from this masterpiece and hasn't permitted me to return to it until this moment, which is two days later. So to continue - I remained at Pearl for several days visiting various maintenance installations, and working out an itinerary with Admiral Pennoyer, who heads up Com-air-pac. In English this means that he is in charge of aircraft mainte- nance in the Pacific. This also included formal requesting from MacArthur that he permit me to visit the Philippines where he is head man and makes no bones about advising everyone of that fact.

Hawaii is one spot that's not overrated. The weather is magnificent. The water is just the right temperature for swimming. And the scenery everything you could ask for. There is always a good sailing breeze, in fact I can imagine no part of the world that could be more ideal for a rest or vacation. We must plan to go into the next San Francisco-Honolulu race.

Traveled from Pearl to Guam by air. This is a long and tiresome trip. It takes from twenty-four to twenty-six hours with two stops for gas and food; one at Johnson island, an atoll 240 ft. long by about 800 feet wide. The runway, naturally, runs the entire length of the island, and it is used solely as a fuelling and air transport check stop, rises about two or three feet above the level of the ocean, and looks as tho'a fair sea would wash it away. The second stop is Kwajelien, a small island in the Marshalls where a similar procedure is followed.

Riding these transports is hard work. They are usually filled to capacity with passengers and freight, and you sit in bucket seats which are extremely hard on the rear end. If you are lucky and quick on your feet you may be able to find room on the deck (floor to you) or a mail bag on which you can attempt to sleep, but usually you have to just grin and bear it. However, it's my understanding that there's a war on and traveling comfort is not a top priority. (Except of course, for friend Eleanor).

The job the air lines are doing in the Pacific theatre is absolutely amazing. They have a network that covers every key island. Regular schedules similar to those at home are maintained, and radio beams have been set up that guide them to their ports of call. They carry passengers, freight, even trucks and bulldozers; in fact, entire naval units with their equipment and rolling stock are often moved from point to point to handle some emergency need.

Guam really isn't too bad. It is far enough north to make the climate bearable. And when I was there the Sea Bees were converting the place into a comfortable base. In fact, I imagine by this time to be stationed on Guam is Good duty (as we say in the Navy). I visited Guam, Saipan and Tinian and then blew south to Ulithy. This consists of a few tiny coral roads that you can scarcely call islands. Its military value lies in the tremendous air strips and maintenance units. I also visited Bill Reed who was on a hospital ship anchored in the lagoon. As a matter of fact, I had lunch with him aboard ship and played a couple of games of gin rummy. He finally beat me at this game, but that was, of course, because I allowed him to do so. (He was low and needed cheering up.)

The next step was Pelelieu, some five air hours farther to the south. This island, as you will remember, was a tough one to take. It's quite hilly and the Japs honeycombed those hills with caves that were impossible to destroy with either shellfire or bombs. The only way to lick them was with foot soldiers who had to burn them out with flame throwers - and that's costly as hell. It proved to be so difficult that it took 72 days to secure the island. (The word secure is used in the Navy in this case instead of take) Judging from maps and newspaper descriptions, Iwo Jima has a similar terrain - and that's not good.

Pelelieu is developing into a major air junction. Planes running to and from the Philippines, from Manus and New Guinea and from the north, all stop there and, because there is also a Marine Air Group stationed on this island that is used to keep the near-by Jap-held island neutralized, the air activity compares in volume with that of LaGuardia field. There is never a time, day or night, when something isn't either warming up, taking off, or landing.

Had a pleasant respite when I left Pelelieu. Instead of making my next jump by air I boarded an L.C.I. and ran out to Kossol Passage. This is about 100 miles distant and on these slow ships is an overnight run. It was a fine tropical night, the sea was smooth, and if your other parent, the great nature lover, had been along, you would have been able to hear her Oh's and Ah's all the way to Annapolis. I snagged a cot, put it out on the deck and had a swell sleep.

Kossel Passage is another lagoon quite similar to the one at Ulithy, and is also used as a harbor by the Navy. At Kossol, however, there is no friendly land nearby as it is hard off the shores of the island of Baudelthraupssol, an island some thirty miles long occupied by a force of 25000 Japs. This force is kept neutralized by the Marine Air Group on Pelelieu who bomb and strafe them daily and, since we have control of the sea and air in this area, they can't do much about it.

In the harbor at Kossol I boarded a sea plane tender. (This is a Naval ship that's used to service sea planes when no shore station is available. It's really too bad that you're not in the Navy so you can understand these terms, but if I haven't made myself clear just let me know and I will be glad to give you further information.) I remained on this ship four days, and was most happy to do so as I was able to have my laundry done. It had developed to a point where I was beginning to dislike even my own smell, and I was becoming sick and tired of C rations. The time spent aboard this tender was most enjoyable. The work they were doing under almost impossible conditions was more than worth the time spent, and there was a grand bunch of guys aboard.

My next stop was to be Manus, an island two degrees south of the equator off the coast of New Guinea, and here again I got a break. There is a major sea plane repair base at Manus and one of the planes with a damaged hull was to be flown there for repairs the day after I finished my job aboard the tender. I was, therefore, able to thumb a ride direct to Manus instead of being forced to go back to Peleliu and follow the transport route.

We were scheduled to take off at four the following morning as the flight takes from eleven to twelve hours. When we went on deck it was not only dark as hell but blowing like the very devil. The job of jumping from the boarding ladder into the bomb loading boat, which is used to get you out to the sea planes, which were anchored astern, was a tough one for the youngsters, who, of course, are no where near as agile as your old man. The boat would come shooting up ten or fifteen feet on top of a wave, then drop down below you an equal distance. The trick, of course, was to jump into the damned thing at just the right moment, and this was quite an operation to perform in the pitch black darkness.

When we got up to the sea plane, we found it too rough to attempt to run alongside so we could climb in. To do so would involve the risk of smashing the side of the plane so they signaled for a large rubber boat, which they most aptly call a worm as it wriggles all over the place in a heavy sea. We then all crawled from the bomb loading boat into the worm, and finally got aboard our sea plane, good and wet, but otherwise none the worse for wear.

We had a grand flight to Manus. I spent a lot of time in the co-pilot's seat, the kids brought along steaks and did a masterful job of cooking them, and we arrived in time for chow (this means dinner) at the air station.

My reasons for going to Manus were twofold. First of all I had to get into MacArthur's domain in order to get into the Philippines. You see, War Correspondents have to be formally accredited to Mr. MacArthur before they can enter his area regardless of whether they have been accepted by the Navy. As a matter of fact three correspondents had the temerity to try it and they were thrown out in short order. So, because I had been accredited to Manus only, I had to go there, and send a dispatch to MacArthur requesting that I be permitted to go to the Philippines. Second, although Manus is a rear area, they very actively support the air arm of the seventh fleet by maintaining a major overhaul operation which repairs aircraft and accessories and I wanted to get the dope on it.

I had to stay on that island for eleven days before I finally received word that I could go to the Philippines. This was most unpleasant. Manus is right smack on the heat equator and no place for a white man. You sweat even in tropical downpours and have only enough energy left to bitch and wish you could get out. However, I did manage to get in some deep sea fishing which was most enjoyable. We went out in a bomb loading boat, one of the guys working in the parachute loft had rigged up some home-made rods, and using lily root, which he dug in the jungle for bait, we caught three fish weighing over thirty pounds each. We would have caught a lot more but for the fact that our rods and tackle were smashed by subsequent strikes. If we had had the proper equipment, we would have brought in some new world's records. There really are fish in those parts, and no mistake.

Well, much to my relief I finally left the Admiralties and flew to Samar in the Philippines via Owi, an island in the Shouten group, and our old friend Pelelieu. At Samar the flight strip had not been completed, so I took a plane to Leyte.

So far as Leyte is concerned you can throw the whole island up for grabs. In short, and in the vernacular of the G.I., it stinks. The weather there is boiling, it rains and you wallow around knee deep in mud, then it's dry for a couple of days and you've got blinding dust. It's the only place where I've experienced both mud and dust at the same time and, I can assure you, the combination is most undesirable. I slept between a rice paddy and a swamp where there were a million different species of bugs and the mosquitoes were real dive bombers.

However, the air strip at Leyte is interesting. It's only about one hundred feet wide and has been built right smack along the water's edge. The available land on either side is so narrow that all aircraft have to be parked wing to wing and there is only about six feet clearance between them to permit a B 24 to land and take off. Consequently, smash ups and crashes were a daily occurrence, and wrecked airplanes were strewn all over the place.

From Leyte I went to Mindoro, one of the islands in the west where we had our most advanced air base. At that time our troops were fighting for Clark Field and were in the outskirts of Manila. The aircraft based at Mindoro, about thirty air minutes away, were furnishing them with bombing and strafing support and also undertaking strikes against Formosa and the China coast.

I was invited to go on one of these trips to the coast, and very foolishly accepted the invitation as they scared hell out of me before I got back. This seemed like a better idea than taking a short trip over Manila, however, as the Japs had been completely shot out of the air over the Philippines and our planes had everything their own way in that entire area.

We left at eight in the morning. We carried a load of bombs, but our major mission was to look for and report enemy ship movements in a sector over the China Sea, to the coast and then down the coast a couple of hundred miles and back to our strip. We flew alone in a Navy P.B.4Y Liberator. When on our way out, perhaps 20 miles off shore, we passed over a fleet of our ships bound for the coast of Luzon. This was quite a sight, and we learned afterwards they were going in on an invasion strike further down the coast. We never went up higher than 2000 feet and I sat in the co-pilot's seat half way over the China Sea, which fact will give you an idea of how well in hand they had the situation at that time.

The relaxed attitude of our pilot and air crew changed completely, however, when we progressed further and I moved back with the waist gunners. This is a grand spot from which to observe. The waist gunners, as you undoubtedly know, shoot from two large open hatches somewhat aft of amidships, and by standing behind them you can see out on either side. When we were some three hundred miles from the China coast we dropped down to within 200 feet of the deck (water to you) so as not to be detected by enemy radar and when land hove in sight I would have been just as glad if we had turned around and gone back home. However it seems that I wasn't in charge of the particular junket, so we kept on and ran right up to the shore.

We then turned south and ran down the beach. At this altitude, as you can well appreciate, we could take in every detail. We flew over fleets of fishing craft, Chinese junks and sampan, but for the most part the shore line was mountainous, bleak and without habitation —- it seemed even further from home to me.

Suddenly we turned, our four engines went on full blast and we dived down to within fifty feet of the deck. To say that we seemed to be going like hell is to indulge in under expression, for with the water this close, 250miles per hour seemed like 2000. After making a run in this fashion for about five minutes, we again turned off on our course, slowed down to cruising speed and climbed back up to two or three hundred feet. That, which from a distance, looked like a large Jap troop transport, had proven to be one of their hospital ships so we didn't attack her. I have thought since that we should have let her have it as she was probably filled with ammunition.

Another fifteen minutes we repeated our former performance. This time it was the real McCoy. The boys had spotted a small cargo ship, and we let her have it. On our approach our bow and crown gunners blasted her until we zoomed up over her stack, then, as we left, our tail gunner gave her the business. Our bombs missed the deck by perhaps two or three feet and hit the water a few feet on her other side, for a near miss. When the wall of water that she threw up subsided we found that she had been thrown around forty-five degrees and was facing towards the shore, she had a heavy list and oil was pouring out of her seams. We circled around once then went on our way, and although we didn't see her sink, she was entirely thru serving the Emperor from that time on.

The rest of the trip was without incident. We flew a total of some two hundred miles down the China Coast, then flew back home. We landed about seven thirty, having been in the air something over eleven hours, and after I got my feet on terra firma again, it seemed to me that the whole trip had been an excellent idea. However, the next time, if there is a next time, I would like to have a job to do. To just stand and look gives one too much time to think and imagine - if you know what I mean.

You really have to experience the distances to appreciate their enormity. The problem of supply is an impossible one, yet they are solving it, and doing a wonderful job at that. The food isn't too bad, in fact in support areas like Manus it's quite good. In newly taken sectors, such as the Philippines when I was there, you get C rations and use mess kits, but such conditions don't last too long.

Discipline is good in forward areas, but the uniform fol de rol that exists in the States is completely dispensed with. The kids wear shorts or skivvies, baseball hats and a pair of G.I. shoes. They have little respect for the Jap as a flyer. He doesn't seem to be able to use his head. The pilot with whom I flew knocked down a Jake on his previous mission without either their pilot or crew seeing him. They didn't know what hit them until they exploded in the air. The same thing seems to hold with their foot soldiers. And if they did not hole up in caves, and make you kill them, they'd be a cinch. However, this suicide characteristic is a tough one. It takes a hell of a long time too kill several million soldiers, and that appears to be the only thing that will stretch out the war.

I think the attitude of the G.I.s in the forward areas is most amusing, especially when it is contrasted with that of the people at home. When we were at Kossol we were with and entire fleet that was anchored within six or seven miles of an island occupied by over twenty thousand Japs, yet the ships were kept blazing with lights every night and movies were shown regularly on the decks of every one of them. The same condition obtains on the islands. Saipan and Guam, for example, each had a thousand or so Japs hiding in the hills and jungles when I was there, yet no one paid any attention to them.

Well, since this is not intended to be the story of my life, and since you undoubtedly have something to do besides read a book on the Pacific, I will bring these ravings to a conclusion. I do hope, however, that you will understand the various navy terms that I have been forced to use, and I feel confident that you will not agree that I should be chief petty officer in charge of type at Madam Gibbs –- So now I will hit the "sack" and "crap off" forthwith.

Dad

*Harvey Conover in South Pacific in 1945
on assignment to review U.S. Navy
aviation maintenance activities*

Bibliography &
Index

BIBLIOGRAPHY

BOOKS

American Battle Monuments Commission, *American Armies and Battlefields in Europe, A History, Guide and Reference Book.* Washington, D.C.: Government Printing Office, 1938.

Boyne, Walter J.; *Silver Wings, A History of the United States Air Force.* New York: Simon & Schuster, 1993.

Brownstone, David; Franck, Irene, *Timelines of War, A Chronology of Warfare from 1000,000 BC to the Present.* Boston: Little Brown and Company, 1994.

Carver, Leland M.; Lindstrom, Gustaf A.; Foster, A. T. *The Ninetieth Aero Squadron, American Expeditionary Forces.* Hinsdale, Ill.: Greist, E. H., 1920.

Clark, Alan. *Aces High, A War in the Air over the Western Front 1914-1917.* New York: G.P. Putnam's Sons, 1973.

Cooke, Jean; Kramer, Ann; Rowland-Entwistle, Theodore. *History's Timeline.* London: Grisewood & Dempsey Ltd., 1981.

Field Service, *The Field Service of the American Ambulance,* described by its members. *Friends of France.* Boston and New York: Houghton Mifflin Company, The Riverside Press-Cambridge, 1916.

Hart, B. H. Captain, *The Real War, 1914-1918.* Norwalk, Connecticut: The Easton Press, 1930, 1958.

Horne, Alistair, *The Price of Glory, Verdun 1916.* Norwalk, Connecticut:

Keegan, John, ed. *The Book of War, 25 Centuries of Great War Writing,* New York, New York: Viking, 1999.

Keegan, John, *The First World War.* Norwalk, Connecticut: The Easton Press, 1998.

Kennett, Lee, *The First Air War, 1914-1918.* New York: The Free Press, A Division of Macmillan, Inc. Toronto, Collier Macmillan Canada, New York, Oxford, Singapore, Sydney, Maxwell Macmillan International, 1991.

Lawson, Eric and Jane, *The First Air Campaign, August 1914-November 1918.* Norwalk Connecticut: The Easton Press, 1996.

Toland, John, *No Man's Land, 1918, The Last Year of the Great War,* Norwalk, Connecticut: The Easton Press, 1980.

Tuchman, Barbara, *The Guns of August,* Norwalk, Connecticut: Easton Press, 1962.

USEFUL INTERNET SOURCES
(All preceded with http://www.)

google.com	theaerodrome.com
info.ox.ac.uk/departments/humanities	hq.nasa.gov/office/pao/history/timeline
lib.utexas.edu/maps/historical/	dean.usma.edu/history/dhistory maps

MAGAZINES AND PERIODICALS

Advertising Magazine. December 13, 1957.

Motor Boating Magazine. February 1958.

Printers Ink Magazine. Volume 13, April 1955, December 13, 1957.

Sports Illustrated Magazine. January 20, 1958.

Yachting Magazine. December 1957, January 1958.

To order additional copies of this book you may contact

Conover-Patterson Publishers
P.O. Box 8647
Spokane, WA 99203-0647
Telephone (509) 624-2829

About Frances C. Church

Fran Church attended Connecticut College from 1941 to 1943. She married Richard Gagney in 1943 and they raised four children. They were divorced in 1970. She returned to college and received her BA from Manhattanville in 1973, and her M.S. from the Columbia School of Social Work in 1976. That same year she joined Family and Children's Services in Stamford, Connecticut as Family Advocate.
This agency received the 1979 Margaret E. Rich Family Advocacy Award from the Family Service Association of America because of the housing coalition Fran developed and implemented under their auspices.

In 1974 she married John Church, a NYC investment banking executive. During the 1980's and 1990's, after they retired, she and John moved to Maine. They made several long-distance cruises by sailboat from Maine to Florida and the Bahamas. They now live in Spokane, Washington. Both enjoy writing and have had material published. They formed Conover-Patterson Publishers in 1996 when they published John's book, *Pasadena Cowboy*.